Dream House,
Real House

Dream House,
Real House

The Adventure of Planning
and Building a Custom Home

Charles J. Daniels

Collier Books
Macmillan Publishing Company
New York

Collier Macmillan Publishers
London

Photographs by Richard P. Daniels

Collier Books
Macmillan Publishing Company
866 Third Avenue, New York, NY 10022
Collier Macmillan Canada, Inc.

Library of Congress Cataloging-in-Publication Data
Daniels, Charles J.
   Dream house—real house: the adventure of planning and building a custom home/by Charles J. Daniels.—1st Collier books ed.
      p.   cm.
   Includes index.
   ISBN 0-02-031230-X
   1. House construction.   2. Architect-designed houses—Design and construction.   I. Title.
   TH4812.D36   1989   89-9886   CIP
   690′.837—dc20

Macmillan books are available at special discounts for bulk purchases for sales promotions, premiums, fund-raising, or educational use.
For details, contact:
Special Sales Director
Macmillan Publishing Company
866 Third Avenue
New York, NY 10022

First Collier Books Edition 1989

10 9 8 7 6 5 4 3 2 1

Printed in the United States of America

CONTENTS

Cast of Characters

Charles Daniels	Owner, Husband
Madeline Daniels	Owner, Wife
Wells	Builder
Binney	Carpenter
Bill	Mason
Greenie	Plumber
Bottle	Drywall
Demper	Electrician
Hagen	Roofer
Brownie	Tile Contractor

"The journey of a thousand miles begins with one step."
                                                    Lao-tse

Foreword

"So just why, after all we've been through, do you want to build another house?" Madeline's voice was a little stressful, and not exactly friendly either. "Besides, the folks down at the real estate office say we're too old to build our dream house." Madeline sells real estate and has done so for the last ten years. "Well," I said, "your dreams and my dreams belong to us, not to them. Besides, selling real estate doesn't necessarily teach you how to turn dreams into a house. It's time for us to build our next dream house, that's why. This house, as comfortable as it is, is too damn big for us now. Sure we filled it up last Christmas with kids and grandkids, but now that I'm going to retire, I don't think this house reflects our life pattern for the future. You know that I'm not retiring just to sit around; you won't have to dust around me in my easy chair. I have other things I want to do and so do you."

"Besides that, there is a lot of profit in this house. We can get at it by selling and building a small, less expensive house. The new house will fit our needs better for the coming years, and the profit we can invest for income during retirement." "Uncle Sam will gobble that up handily," she snapped, adding, "dinner is about ready." "Not true," I said, "I have it figured out so we won't lose one cent of the profit to income taxes." "All right! *All right!*" Madeline said. "Prove it to me and dinner is now ready!" The husband always gets the last two words. "Yes, dear."

"Let's move into a condo and I'll rent a barn or old garage for my craft work," I remarked. "Absolutely not," said Madeline, "just get the idea out of your head. I want you here so we can be together, not off somewhere in an old barn." "How about a town house or an apartment?" "Absolutely not!" she quipped. "Well then," I surmised, "I guess that means a new house." Then she said thoughtfully, "We are not so young anymore; what happens should one of us get sick?" I answered, "You could have asked *that* question when we first got married. I hereby proclaim, regardless of what you think, that we are both unusually healthy and that we can probably count on that continuing for the next, hmmmm, say fifteen years! I admit that should I be wrong, we must have contingency plans, but what if I am right? Do we wait around for the difficult times? I vote for the good times." Quietly she said, "Let's go for the good times." "All right," I said, "let's go for building a new custom house for us." "You wanted to do that anyway," she said.

"Castles in the air are all right 'till we try to move into them."
Author Unknown

1
Dream House, Real House

This is the story of the fourth house my wife and I built. I tell it from the viewpoint I know — that of the owner. There are so many people involved in building a house that the owner's view often gets lost. Yet through the years that follow it is the owner who lives with the comforts, the good things, the bad things, the mistakes. In any event, he usually pays for them year after year.

Here is a detailed account of the planning, the purchase of a lot, the custom design of the house to go on that lot, the approach to getting the house up, the day by day events, the expenditures, and finally, AH! moving in. I am, for sure, much more involved in these activities than most people want to be. If you dream of your custom home, however, it is better to know about these events even if you never get deeply involved. The dream comes truer that way.

Rewards and risks come with building a custom home. There is much to be said for buying an existing house because it eliminates some of the risk. This is especially true when the owner's life savings are involved. If the risks of building your custom dream house seem overwhelming, and the financial burden will leave you marginal, reconsidering is in order. After all, a mis-step under these conditions destroys the dream.

1

Most builders will tell you that building even the simplest house is still a bit of an adventure. Those appealing ads in magazines about beautiful floors, darling decorations, precious nurseries, great roofs, skylights, and hot tubs have a place but I find them mostly frustrating. They somehow have to be pieced together if the owner is to get what he needs, and ads don't help much in that department. Much of the material in published ads is there to ensnare the owner and frequently it avoids revealing what the owner needs to know most—where do the risks lurk and how can he manage or avoid them? There are lucky breaks, negotiations, accidents, weather, building inspections, price changes, mistakes, conflicts among subcontractors and even some pretty big unknowns such as digging a well. Yet the dream of building one's own custom home goes on. It should go on. You should know that when you bring together sound information and knowledge, the risks can be managed and your custom dream home can become a reality.

I have not just chronicled the events of this, our latest custom home, but I have also, with each step along the way, given my own view of things. Certainly every reader will not agree with my views. I hope, however, that my views will stir your thoughts and bring you a step closer to realizing *your* dream house.

§

"It takes a heap o' living in a house t' make it a home."
Edgar A. Guest

Instant nostalgia—yes it's available in a dream house! Buy an old house and rehabilitate it. This can be done and we all have seen some beautiful examples. The work of rehabbing an old house is, however, usually much more than the owner realizes and frequently an inferior dream house results. Basic room sizes may be inadequate for today's activities. Most old houses were built before the days of truss roofs and accordingly partitions can't be moved around at will lest the house fall down. Original plumbing and electrical installations are poor by today's standards and are very expensive to replace. Also modern heating and air conditioning equipment is hard to install in an old house. If one is determined to go this route, needless to say, selection of a rehabbable house is a most important first step. An excellent book on this subject is *This Old House* by Bob Vila and Jan Davison (Little Brown and Co., Boston). The second house we owned was an oldie and, after rehabbing it, I decided that new construction was the way for me to go.

Love those movies and TV shows where the family house is a given; it's solid and forever. Perhaps Southfork and the Ponderosa really were that way, but alas, they alone were. Today for whatever reason, most of us move about and our homes get sold, then sold again. More important than that, most of us end up with life savings tied up in our homes, and life savings are something to hang onto when selling. If one works at it, the sale may even be profitable. So as history marches onward, the dream of the dream house keeps changing. Excluding our new home, about which this book is written, my wife and I have owned five homes and we have had to sell all of them. Someday the new house will have to be sold too. All of these were sold at a profit, but for the last four, there has been no income tax paid on the gain. In fact, if one meets certain conditions, Uncle Sam will no longer allow you to pay tax on profit from the sale of your home! The tax is deferred until some indefinite time in the future. Internal Revenue Service publication 523 *Tax Information on Selling Your Home* tells it all.

 Department of the Treasury
Internal Revenue Service

Publication 523

Tax Information on Selling Your Home
Introduction

This publication explains the basis of a home, how you may postpone the tax on part or all of the gain on the sale of your home, and how you may exclude part or all of the gain from your gross income if you are 55 or older.

§

There is the concept of the custom "turn key" house. Some really need to have a "turn key." The concept is that the house is perfect in all respects when the owner moves in—all he needs to do is turn the key and start living it up. No matter how much money is poured into it, the "turn key" is only a concept and can only be partly achieved. There are those whose job or social demands do not permit spending time to complete or perfect a new house, and they need a "turn key." They may miss something in life, but then perhaps they gain it on the other end.

3

I have always found it rewarding to myself and my family to work on my home. It can also be financially rewarding. For example, when you have the local contractor install your automatic garage door opener (not too tough a job), you have to earn the money to pay him. You must first, however, pay tax on the money you earn, and with what's *leftover* you may pay him. Then too, you will have to pay his markup on the materials plus his profit on the job. He will do the job faster than you but if you have the time you will be ahead. Your family's standard of living will improve, and if you were careful, the value of your house will go up. Your profit will be locked into your house, and when you sell (someday you will) you may pay no tax on the profit. Be selective and work on things that will improve the value of your house. The garage door opener is only an easy example. Should you be a lawyer, carpenter, architect, nursery man or any other—do your thing.

§

In order to understand this book thoroughly you must now take a few minutes reading to understand what our situation was before we started to build and how we went about coping with the various factors that went into building our new "dream house." *You* also have a very individual situation which needs considering. The hope is that you will learn by transferring as much pertinent information from our experience, which has been reasonably successful, to yours.

When we bought our first house we had one baby, a son. At that time I dreamed of a beautiful little cottage. When we bought our second house we had two children, a boy and a baby girl. I dreamed of a not too big but bigger home. Our third house (the first house we built) found us with three children, and I dreamed of entertaining friends and business associates, as well as young people gathering at our house. When we built our next house, we had four children and I dreamed of further entertaining, high school proms, and college students. There was only one child at home when we built our fifth house and our requirements had changed again. The dream goes on, but it changes and so do the requirements for a dream home.

Now we come to house number six. Life found me newly retired. It was the first time we needed to build a smaller instead of a larger home. This may seem like a big change, but it was not. The activities and action principles were the same for the first house we built as this new one. One dramatic change had taken place though, and that was in the area of government rules and taxes. Be sure you understand these before building your dream home or else the dream just might not come true. Because the profit from the sale of each of our houses had been transferred to the next, in accordance with tax regulations, we had paid no tax on this profit. The result was that our home was fully paid for and free of any mortgage. It was clear that we would get the money to build our new home from selling the old one but there was a tax problem with this. I wanted to transfer *all* the profit from the sale of the house to the new house so that again, no tax would be due. To do this, according to tax regulations, the *purchase price* of the new house must be greater than the *sale price* of the old house. No, there isn't much logic to it, it's just the way the regulation is.

The glitch was that we wanted to build a smaller less expensive house. If we did that, we would have to pay tax on the difference between the sale price and the purchase price, provided there was at least that much profit from the sale (which there was).

Example: Sale price of old house	$300,000
Purchase price of new house	-$200,000
Amount on which tax would have to be paid	$100,000

> *"Over and over again the courts have said that there is nothing sinister in so arranging one's affairs as to keep taxes as low as possible. Everybody does so, rich or poor; and all do right, for nobody owes a public duty to pay more than the law demands. Taxes are enforced extractions, not voluntary contributions."*
> Judge Learned Hand

Sometimes it's better to be older. Not many years ago the government passed another tax law having to do with the sale of homes by persons 55 years or older. This subject is also covered in IRS Publication 523. When such an oldie sells his home he may keep (only once in his life) the profit from the sale up to $125,000 *tax free*! Oh yes, the profits from the sale of the previous homes count and all add up. This applies to singles and married couples as if they were one person. Rulings on this when divorce and re-marriage are involved are something else and are worth reading just for the amusing confusion. No, there isn't much logic to the whole thing; just read and believe. The previous example calculation now becomes:

Sale price of house	$300,000
Once in a lifetime forgiven profit	-$125,000
No tax due if new house, including lot, costs more than this amount	$175,000

My rough cut at the cost of a new smaller house was around $200,000 (including lot and building cost) which easily exceeds the $175,000. Think about it for a moment and you will see that the closer we could come to the $175,000 figure for the new house costs, the more tax free cash we could keep to invest for income. I thought that we could not build and get into a new house for the magic $175,000 figure, but that we could achieve a substantial part of that goal should the cost be in the $200,000 range. We decided to take our once in a lifetime tax benefit as part of our dream house plan. The remainder of the profit, if any, would be transferred to the new home and we would have no income tax to pay on the profit. The old house finally sold for a little over $300,000. So the plan was set:

- Buy a building lot to our liking.
- Sell our present house — then we would know for sure how much money would be available to build the new house.
- Find and move into a rented house near the building lot. We considered building first, then selling, and moving directly into the new house. This entailed more risk and I was not comfortable with the plan. So we rented and took the beating of moving twice. P.S. It took a year to sell the old house.
- Develop house plans to accommodate our needs and to fit the lot.
- Find at least two qualified builders and get estimates of cost. Then with the best information available, select the builder.
- Set a practical plan for payments during construction — one that would be agreeable to us, the builder and the money lending institution, if one were involved.
- Build the house and pay for it.
- Move in (Hooray!)
- Complete chores after moving in.

2
A Lot To
Build Upon

I lived in a house once where the basement was subject to flooding. Everytime we got a drenching rain, I got a little apprehensive wrench in the gut — year in and year out. Most county codes require a sump pump in such basements. The automatic pump, which runs on electricity, is located in a sump well below the basement floor, and it pumps local water out before it gets high enough to flood. Water entering the basement from anywhere else is supposed to drain over the floor and into the sump well. Now, power outages are common during thunderstorms, heavy rain, and local flooding. Then, just when needed most, the sump pump doesn't work at all. A ground level walk-out basement is a good answer to this problem but it does usually require a lot sloping away from the road. The front of the house (facing the road) is at ground level while the basement floor and door at the back are also at ground level. Such basements seldom have need for a sump pump. If a pipe bursts, water will accumulate on the basement floor and run out the basement door before heavy flooding occurs. A sailor would call it self-bailing. Because the outside ground level at the back is at, or below, the basement floor, some good sized windows in the basement are quite feasible, thus yielding the common name "daylight basement." When properly constructed, daylight basements are much less prone to condensation and mildew — in fact, light and airy basements are possible. Little wonder then that I prefer a lot which permits a house design with a walk-out daylight basement.

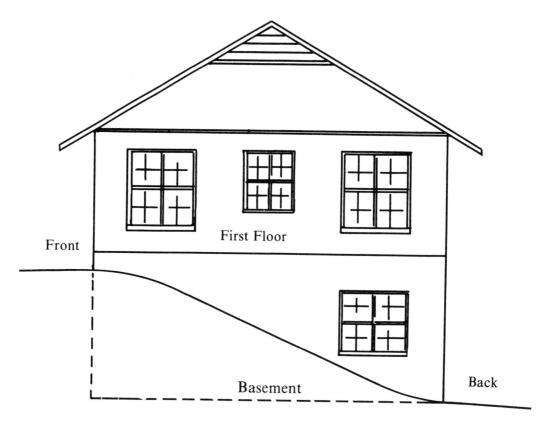

Front

First Floor

Basement

Back

The front and the back of the house is essentially at ground level, providing a light and airy first floor as well as a light and airy basement.

There are many places where basements are not feasible, usually where the land is level and the water table is only a few feet below the surface. Here, houses are frequently built on concrete slabs raised above the ground. In comparison, the extra space provided by a basement is expensive when incorporated into a one story basementless house. Nevertheless slab house designs do circumvent the wet basement problem. These comments also apply to conventional basementless houses where the floor is constructed on floor joists raised above the ground.

I just won't get much agreement on the subject of trees. A sparsely treed lot I find to be all right, but a heavily treed lot is not so desirable. Too many trees cause a home to be dark inside and frequently inhibit ventilation making the house musty. Then too, trees that are dangerously close to the house may fall and cause property damage and injuries to people. When a house is built, the moisture pattern for the ground under and around it is drastically changed. There is nothing certain about this, but nearby trees may die. Established trees may take five years to give up and then the *owner* has another problem. In all, I prefer to plant my own trees where they will serve me well. Like my father, I am a gardener, and must provide for a garden spot where the sun shines in. Heavily treed lots don't permit this and I count that as a negative. So it comes about that I prefer an open lot, or a lightly treed lot. Please don't suggest that a treed lot be cleared because, if permitted at all by local covenants, neighbors won't like you for that!

Exposure to the sun has received much attention lately, and of course, orientation of the lot dictates much about the exposure of the house. Solar heating buffs will want to spend considerable time on this matter but I have found that selection of a lot involves many other important aspects. After all, one side of the house will face near south whether one likes it or not. And if the long side of the house faces south then the opposite side will face north, a point worth considering if the north side is exposed to winter winds. My preference is to position picture windows (and other windows in daytime living areas) to face the best view available and this just may not be to the south. So, in all, I count a southern exposure as desirable but not essential.

Since buying a lot and putting up a custom house is a hugh expenditure, be prudent when selecting a lot; pick one where the value will appreciate. Easier said than done! Only you will know your personal requirements (such as it must be within automobile commuting distance from your job) and these may in the end dominate your choice. My simple view of a lot that will appreciate includes these features: the area should not be fully built up but some houses should already be completed; the quality, nature and cost of the homes being built there should generally be in the same range you seek. The land in the area should be appropriately subdivided and zoned so that favorable custom residential building will likely take place; you must be able to visualize the area as being attractive to the general public when finally built up. This way the desirability of the neighborhood has already been established before you buy. Should you build your own home there, you can contribute further to that thrust. If after you buy you decide not to build (one can't outguess everything) you may be able to sell the lot for the same price you paid for it or maybe even a little more. On the other hand you may want to just hold on to it as an investment if the conditions look favorable.

It took about three years of looking before we found the right lot. By then we had narrowed the specific areas which interested us to two or three. Madeline brought home weekly reports from her real estate files about new lots as they became available. Those that seemed promising we explored over the weekends. The lot we selected is in the Northern Virginia area and is counted as a suburb of Washington D.C. It is within easy driving distance of the D.C. and other business centers in Virginia, and only a little over a mile from the local shopping center. Some beautiful homes had already been built nearby when we bought. The development was in a country setting and had horse riding centers nearby.

County authorities here rule with a heavy hand and when an area is subdivided into building lots it must be submitted first for their approval. Lots in this area are, so to speak, in the country (city water and sewer are not available) and it is necessary to have a well, septic tank and drain field. Perk tests to establish the water absorbtion capability of the land are required. The county establishes the placement of the well and the size and the position of the septic tank and drain field. I asked a county health authority how he could put a spot on a map and say that's exactly where the well should be. How did he know that we would strike water at that spot? I know that it's not that easy in some other counties. He said that if we didn't get water, it would be the first time in these parts. He was right! These county selections can be appealed and adjusted if the county agrees.

I found, for most of the lots available, the county had positioned the house building site and the drain field so that the effluent from the septic tank must be pumped by electric pump up to the drain field, which subsequently distributes it to be absorbed into the ground. Although approved by the county, I still don't like the arrangement. We have power outages from time to time and I don't know what they do about that. I prefer the water/sewage to drain naturally by gravity from the house to the septic tank and then to the drain field. Gravity is one hundred percent reliable and requires no maintenance. I'm for that. Most of the lots I thought worth looking into had to be pumped, so I rejected them.

One day I was driving through an area I considered desirable and I saw a "Lot for Sale" sign. Walking a number of yards down a gravel lane I made my way through some brush into an open field. Stakes in the corners gave me a clue as to the lot size. It sloped in the right direction all right, but not as much as I would have liked.

A phone call to the number on the "For Sale" sign soon brought us to the real estate office offering the property. We found out that it was a two acre lot in a subdivision of lots. The boundaries had already been established and approved by the county as were the perk tests, septic tank and drain field, well and building locations. Pumping was not required. Since he was right there at the real estate office, I talked to the architect who had laid out the subdivision and was familiar with county codes. I told him I wanted to put a daylight basement house on the lot with one bathroom on the basement floor level. He was skeptical about it because the lot did not have much slope. If the front of the house at first floor level were positioned to look right (about twenty inches above the finished land level), then the basement floor (about nine feet below the first floor), might be too deep in the ground for the downstairs bath to drain into the septic tank. On the other hand, if the basement floor were set high enough for the bath to drain properly into the septic tank, the front of the house might look awkwardly high out of the ground. He said that if a bathroom were to be placed at basement floor level, a pump for just that one bath might be practical. I thanked him and said I would check it out.

§

Years ago I attended the Canal Zone Junior College — my family lived in the Panama Canal Zone. I spent two summers working as a surveyor-helper for the Canal Zone Section of Surveys. One summer was spent developing the annual survey of the Panama Canal. In those days slides and canal blockages still happened occasionally, although nowhere near as much as when the canal was first opened. I spent a second summer locating and accurately positioning anti-aircraft gun locations in the wilderness around the Canal locks. Except for the bugs, those were great summers and I learned a lot about surveying.

Now, at last, those summer experiences were going to pay off. I bought a site level (a poor man's surveyor level) and went to work figuring out the lay of the land. Madeline held the rod (a long stick with feet and inches marked on it) at various places while I "shot" the elevations. My numbers confirmed the county's contour map within a few inches, which is remarkable since they get their information from aerial photographs. It worked out that, if I added some fill dirt in the front yard, and sloped the land upward slightly from the road to the house (the natural ground slope was the opposite), I could squeeze in the basement level bath with good drainage to the septic tank.

We were ready to make a bid on the lot. The lot was advertised at $55,000. We went to the sales agent, and I explained that the gravel roadway had a 50 foot easement along the lot line, and since we can't build on an easement, the true useful area of the lot was much less than the advertised two acres. Further, the lot was already long and narrow and the fifty foot easement narrowed it even more, making it difficult to accomodate house dimensions plus county space restrictions for the septic tank and drain field. Other lots in the subdivision were not so restricted. In any case I felt that the lot should not command the advertised price, and we offered $50,000. The contract was written at our price and offered to the sellers. A few days later the sellers countered at $51,500. We signed and the lot was ours. After the various cost adjustments for settlement, we paid a total of $52,067.99.

The next page is a copy of the actual settlement sheet the settling attorney provided us (names omitted). It reveals the items considered by the attorney and exactly how much we paid for each item. Madeline advised that, since we were not placing a loan on the lot and the attorney had little to do (type up papers, sign and record the transaction at the county court house), his charge of $468.50 was a bit much. I pointed out the unusual credit of $165.08 for "early settlement" and we decided not to argue the point.

We had known for several years that we were going to buy a lot at the first good opportunity. During this time we arranged our finances and built up a separate account for the purpose of buying the lot. When the time came to pay, we were prepared and bought it for cash, that is, without resorting to a loan. This was done before our house was sold and we had to temporarily stretch and strain some other finances in order to make the payment. When the house was sold, the stretching and straining ended and our finances were restored to normal. It's worth noting that there were no loan fees or points to pay and thereby settlement costs were minimized.

At the time we purchased our lot, other two acre lots in the subdivision had been selling in the $80,000 to $100,000 range. How did it happen that we were able to purchase our two acre lot for $52,000? First, although surrounded by trees, our lot was open. The other lots were beautifully treed and there is no question that people will pay more for a treed lot. There is another important point that also applies here. Our lot was not an easy lot to build on and most buyers sensed this. They sensed it, but they didn't grasp the problem securely and then they did the smart thing for them, they didn't offer to buy. It happened that we could handle the specific problems, and when we felt we had the problems securely tied down, we bid. It happened and I'm glad.

J. SUMMARY OF PURCHASER/BORROWER'S TRANSACTION			K. SUMMARY OF SELLER'S TRANSACTION		
100.	GROSS AMOUNT DUE FROM BORROWER:		400.	GROSS AMOUNT DUE TO SELLER:	
101.	Contract sales price	51,500.00	401.	Contract sales price	51,500.00
102.	Personal property		402.	Personal property	
103.	Settlement charges to borrower *(line 1400)*	468.50	403.	Extras	
104.	Purchase of escrow funds		404.	Sale of escrow funds	
105.			405.		
Adjustments for items paid by seller in advance:			*Adjustments for items paid by seller in advance:*		
106.	City/town taxes to		406.	City/town taxes to	
107.	County taxes 5/12/83 6/30/83	99.49	407.	County taxes to	
108.	Assessments to		408.	Assessments to	
109.	Rental to		409.	Rental to	
110.	PMI/FHA Ins. to		410.	PMI/FHA Ins. to	
111.			411.		
120.	GROSS AMOUNT DUE FROM BORROWER:	52,067.99	420.	GROSS AMOUNT DUE TO SELLER:	51,500.00
200.	AMOUNTS PAID BY OR IN BEHALF OF BORROWER:		500.	REDUCTIONS IN AMOUNT DUE TO SELLER:	
201.	Deposit or earnest money BHR	1,000.00	501.	Deposit held by Seller	
202.	Principal amount of new loan(s)		502.	Settlement charges to seller *(line 1400)*	3,398.00
203.	Existing loan(s) taken subject to		503.	Existing loan(s) taken subject to	
204.	Purchase Money Trust from Seller		504.	Purchase Money Trust to Purchaser	
205.			505.	Payoff of first trust loan Hanes	36,050.00
206.			506.	Payoff of second trust loan	
207.			507.	Clerk's fee - Release of	
208.			508.	first trust	3.50
209.	Credit for early settlement	165.08	509.	Credit for early settlement	165.08
Adjustments for items unpaid by seller:			*Adjustments for items unpaid by seller:*		
210.	City/town taxes to		510.	City/town taxes to	
211.	County taxes to		511.	County taxes 1/1/83 to 5/12/83	260.66
212.	Assessments to		512.	Assessments to	
213.	Rental to		513.	Rental to	
214.	Interest to		514.	Interest to	
215.	PMI/FHA Ins. to		515.	PMI/FHA Ins. to	
216.			516.		
220.	TOTAL PAID BY/FOR BORROWER:	1,165.08	520.	TOTAL REDUCTION AMOUNT DUE SELLER:	39,877.24
300.	CASH AT SETTLEMENT FROM/TO BORROWER:		600.	CASH AT SETTLEMENT TO/FROM SELLER:	
301.	Gross amount due from borrower *(line 120)*	52,067.99	601.	Gross amount due to seller *(line 420)*	51,500.00
302.	Less amounts paid by/for borrower *(line 220)*	(1,165.08)	602.	Less reductions in amount due seller *(line 520)*	(39,877.24)
303.	CASH (X FROM) (☐ TO) BORROWER:	50,902.91	603.	CASH (X TO) (☐ FROM) SELLER:	11,622.76

LOT PURCHASE
SETTLEMENT SHEET

THE LOT TO BUILD UPON
LOT SIZE AND ORIGINAL TOPOGRAPHY

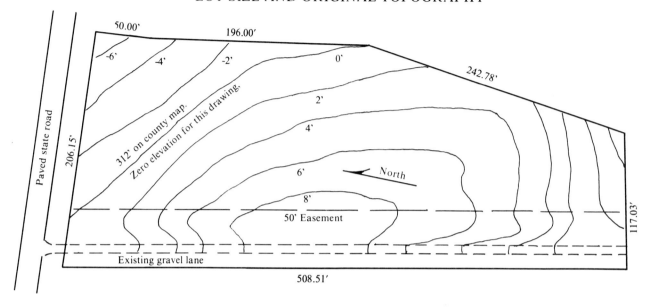

Zero elevation for this drawing, same as 312' on county map.

For those not familiar with topography (contour line) drawings: imagine the lot flooded with water to the 0' level. The contour line on the drawing would be exactly the same as the water shore line. Then raise the water level by two feet— the shore line would then be the same as the 2' contour line, and so on for 4', 6', 8' etc.

FINAL TOPOGRAPHY

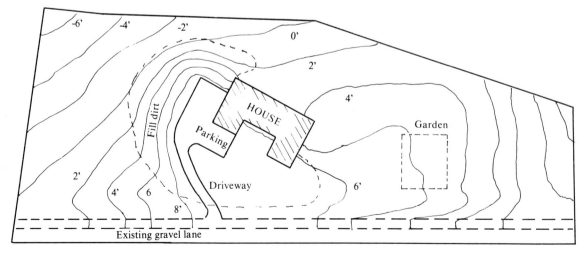

"We should learn from the snail: it has devised a home that is both exquisite and functional."

Frank Lloyd Wright

3
House Plans, Maybe More Than You Think

When I left the Panama Canal Zone I was twenty-one. I was born there of parents from New York State and of U.S. citizenship. I had a choice of citizenship and without hesitation it was U.S., although I have always thought fondly of Panama. I went to the University of Michigan, Ann Arbor, where I had been accepted in the Engineering College to obtain a degree in Naval Architecture. Having graduated from the two year Canal Zone Junior College, it would take five semesters to graduate from Michigan. It was a big change for me, not only was seeing my breath in the air an intriguing novelty, I had never seen snow — man, did I see snow! I graduated with a BSE in Naval Architecture, but as it happened, I never once worked in a shipyard.

Ships carry people too, and some of my education at Michigan had to do with rooms to live in, dining areas, passageways, kitchens, storage areas, etc. A

15

surprising amount of this education transfers to the design of houses. I am still taken aback when I see brand new homes or even public buildings with inadequate passageways, clearances, and traffic patterns. This usually results from the designer's attempt to attain some dramatic or aesthetic effect. The trick of course, is to obtain both. Nature's geometry does not always allow for both and when this is the case, I almost always opt for the easier living pattern.

When the time came to build our first custom house, I decided to do the design, drafting, drawings, and specifications on my own. Madeline and I had some great discussions about our future and what the house should accomodate. I learned things about her and she about me. Prominent in our discussions was the question, "What if we ever had to sell?" With our life savings going into this house, we saw that it was risky to incorporate into the design those personal quirks which might be attractive to us but not marketable. A leveling and sobering thought.

Eventually I found a brave pencil and put our ideas all down on paper. When the plans were finished, I took them to a local architect who did custom homes and spent three hours with him going over the details. He suggested a different pattern of glass at the entrance and that some doors be hinged to the left instead of the right — suggestions which I incorporated. He congratulated me on a nice design. I paid his fee and left with a lot more confidence under my belt than when I entered.

Less than twelve months after the house was built I had a fine job offer in another city. We sold the house and moved. Before getting to our latest house, the course of life would bring me to design, build, and live in two more. That latter point "and live in" is something I suspect many architects never experience. It's worth a lot.

My first approach to designing a new house is to make small scale floor plan sketches to a scale 1/8 inch to the foot. I don't get much in final house dimensions out of these, but if I can get Madeline to look at them, I get some pretty strong positive and negative reactions which I use for guidance. Once she surprised me by looking over my shoulder and asking how it was coming. I remarked, "If you can put up with a bow, a stern, and a poop deck, we're gonna be okay."

Working with geometric patterns, which is what happens when one attempts to lay out house plans, is a revealing experience. We are all indeed confined to God's geometry, and this does not ever conform to a man's idea for a perfect house plan. Being extravagant with floor area (or expensive features) does not change this one bit. In the end, the best layout draftsman or architect in the world is forced to compromise some wanted features. My approach is to work and re-work plans until the compromises between what I seek and what geometry allows are minimized.

I decided that I wanted to have a "great-room" this time, no formal dining room or lame living room. Just one big room for living, dining, fireplace, TV and stereo. Madeline agreed that great-rooms were currently quite popular. She had sold some houses with great-rooms, and they were not only acceptable but in fact she liked them. I knew that a great-room would cut down on the size of the house and that was a goal I wanted to achieve. There was a problem here though; the convenants required a minimum of 2300 square feet of living space and that was pushing me into a bigger house than I thought we needed.

When a parcel of land is split up into building lots, the county ordinances and regulations have first say. The county can insist on anything from limiting lot size to forbidding building on a flood plain. In addition, the subdivider of the land can add to these restrictions; for example, all houses must be two story or a minimum number of square feet. Owner restrictions are called covenants and must be adhered to.

We had decided to design an "all-on-one-floor" house. The covenant requirement of 2300 square feet, however, is not quite a small house for two people when placed on one floor. I resolved this by placing a bedroom, closets and bath on the basement level. We may seldom use these rooms, and they may not get cleaned regularly; but they helped to meet the covenant. Also, should we have to sell, the house would be more acceptable to the marketplace.

After much push and pull on the small sketches, we arrived at our decision. It would be a daylight basement rambler with necessary living accomodations for two people all on one floor. The plans would call for: a large master bedroom with bath, a guest room and hall bath, a great-room for living and dining, a good size kitchen with desk and eating space for two, a pantry, and a laundry room next to the kitchen in a small "work room." A screened porch would also be located directly next to the kichen. Madeline insisted on a side-loading garage and this added about 600 cubic yards of fill dirt to make the driveway functional. A full basement would give me a large workshop for my craft activities and would also include a little-used one bedroom suite with bath. All that having been decided I set up a drafting table and went to work drawing the actual house plans. By this time we had sold our house and moved into a rental nearby the building site.

It took about sixty days to complete the house plans. A tremendous amount of information goes into these plans, and no designer gets it all absolutely correct. The best you can do is get the dimensions correct and provide enough information so that people in the trades, the ones who actually build the house, know what you want. Too much detail can actually confound the situation. There must, on the other hand, be enough information to obtain county approval and a county building permit. I got the final plans on only four drawings. A copy of these, simplified and reduced in size, are given here.

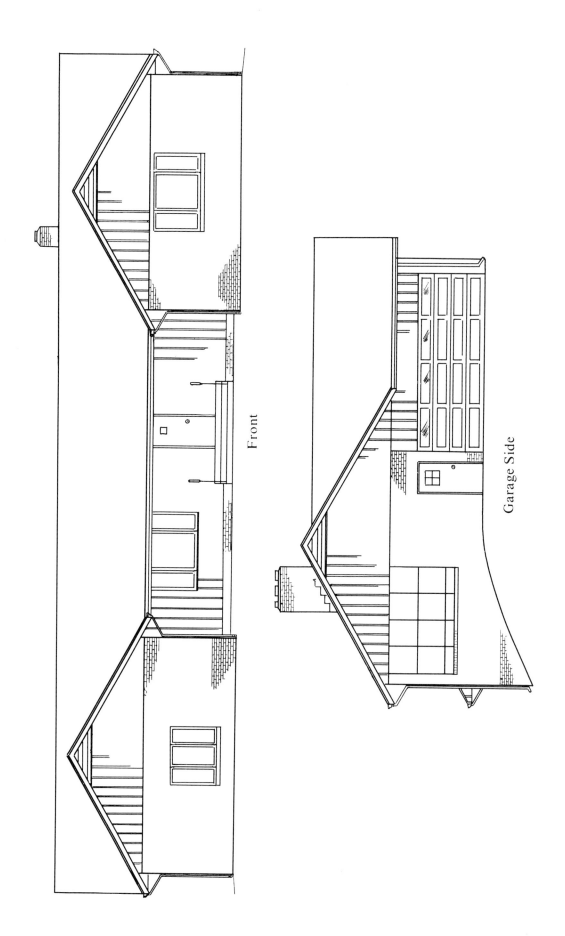

Front

Garage Side

18

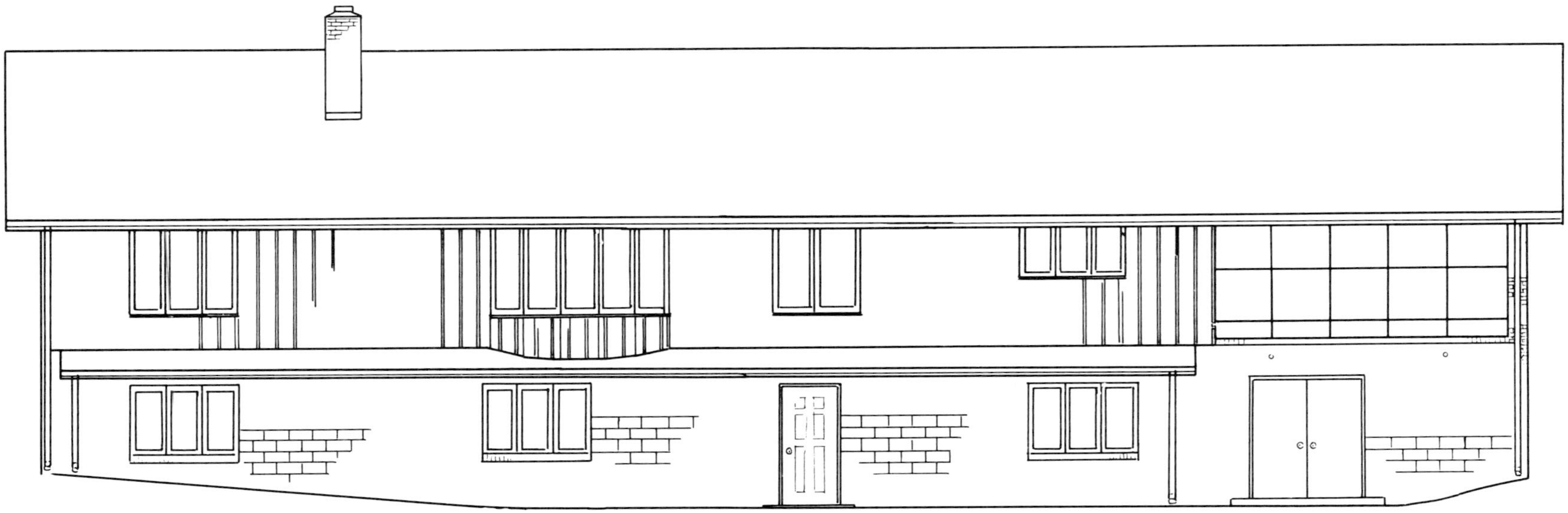

Back

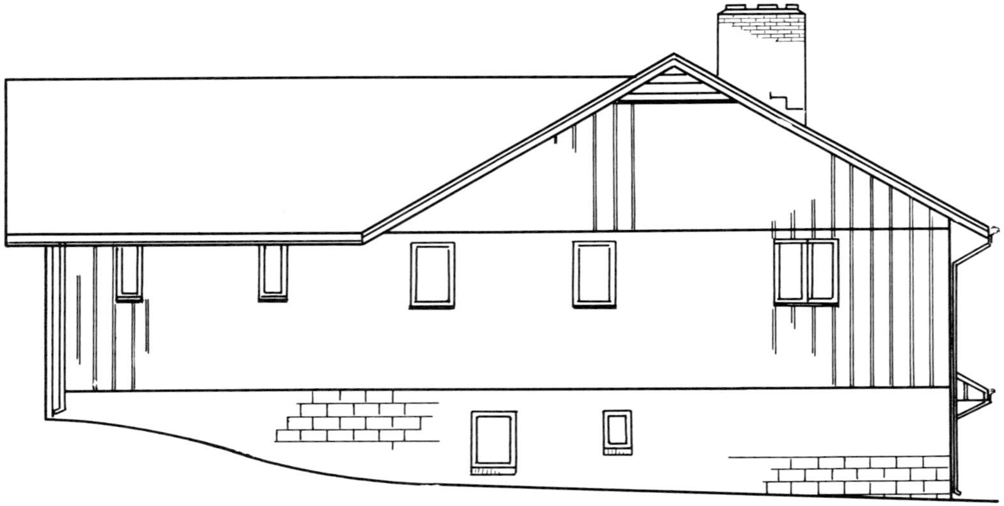

Bedroom Side

HOUSE PLANS

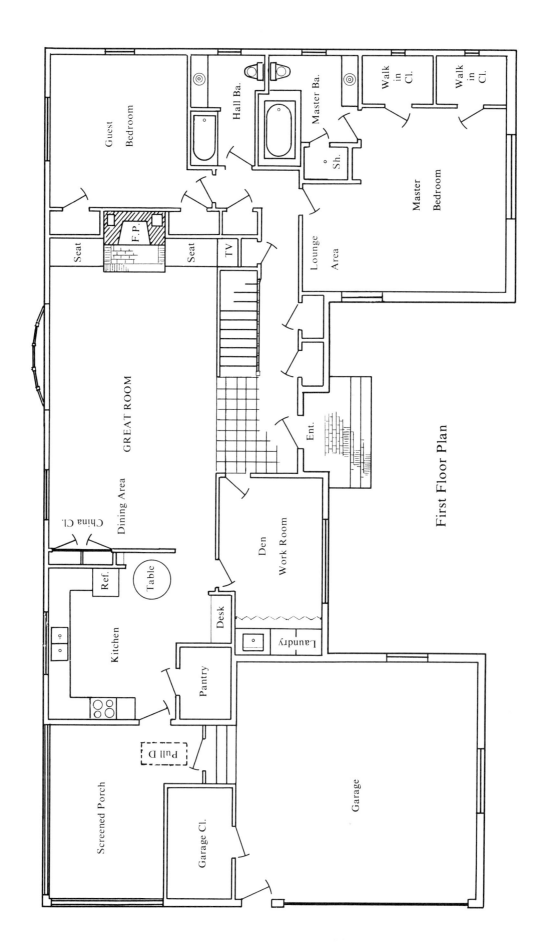

First Floor Plan

20

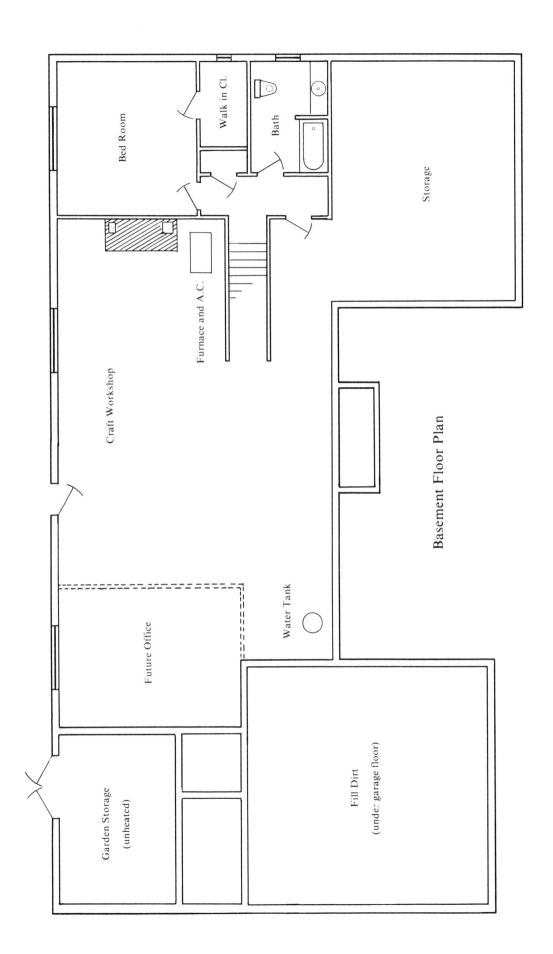

Bed Room

Walk in Cl.

Bath

Craft Workshop

Furnace and A.C.

Storage

Future Office

Water Tank

Garden Storage
(unheated)

Fill Dirt
(under garage floor)

Basement Floor Plan

HOUSE PLANS

21

The way I generate house plans is probably not practical for other house dreamers. Many builders offer a service of drawing custom house plans. Another option is to find a house plan that sort of fits you and make a few personal adjustments. Several house magazines sell "complete" sets of house plans which are suitable for this approach. If you go this path, arrive at the builder's table with as complete a design as you can. Chances are, he will suggest changes particularly to reduce costs. Then if he does the final plans, he will at least know what's in them.

Do you need an architect? Public buildings and the like need an architect. Here we are concerned about an individual home. I don't see how a good architect can take time to learn your individual likings in the detail you need, put them down in house plans, and still make a living. Should you want a stylized house accurately portraying features of some historical period, I believe an architect could be very helpful. He will know how to research the subject even if he does not deal every day in your selected house style. For an individual home, however, your builder will know about house plans, county licenses, county codes, structures, supplies, etc., and he will help you to incorporate these aspects into your plans. Be cautious, however, for the builder (or architect) may or may not have much feel for aesthetics. You should double check this aspect of your plans to make sure you will get what you expect.

Go over every aspect of the house plans in detail before you release them to the builder. Avoid the idea that changes can be made to suit as the house goes up. Such changes almost always cost more than quoted prices. Take the builder's advice if you wish and make changes before the final go-ahead, but try to avoid them afterward. Even after the most scrupulous efforts, some changes inevitably must be made as construction progresses. Think before you speak.

Before leaving the subject of house plans, I should comment on the conservation of energy. Previously I mentioned that it is usually impractical to select an ideal lot for solar warmth. So it was with our lot, but that does not stop one from using the best of what one has. The back of the house, the two story side, faces southeast and is drenched in sunlight in winter until about noon. This side of the house has by far the most window area and accepts the warmth and light from the winter sun. In summer it still gets a lot of sunlight, but because the sun is positioned further north and rises more rapidly than in winter, the heat of the day is cut off early by the two foot roof overhang. The northern side of the house is partly shielded from winter winds by the garage and also by the row of trees, which are not evergreen, along the lane leading to the driveway.

Exterior walls of the house are framed with two by six inch studs permitting two extra inches of insulation compared to standard two by four inch studs. All windows are double glazed, that is, they have two panes of glass with an air space between, giving a much better insulative condition than single glazing. A heavy layer of insulation blown into the attic resists heat loss through the ceiling. The builder suggested that I move the attic pull down stairway to some uninsulated area because "it causes a break in the attic insulation." I moved the pull down to the uninsulated screened porch ceiling where it functions very well. Now the police tell me that the house is more vulnerable to thieves because they can cut the screen, enter the attic through the pull down, and break through the ceiling to enter the house. You can't win 'em all. The house design lends itself nicely to vaulted ceilings and skylights. These faddish features are flagrant losers of heat in the winter although they may have some merit in keeping the house cooler in summer. I resisted these "latest styles" and incorporated an unbroken insulation blanket in the attic over living areas which translates into a flat unbroken ceiling in the house.

HOUSE POSITION ON LOT

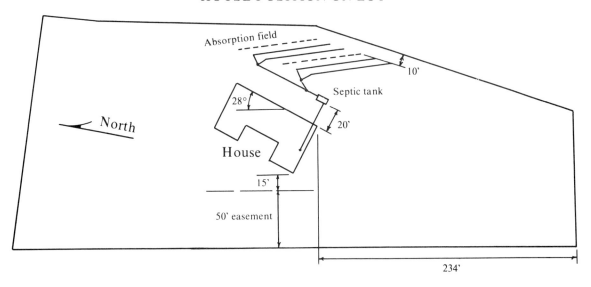

The county required provision for six drain lines in the absorption field, each seventy-two feet long, spaced six feet apart, and no closer than ten feet from any property line. Four of these lines were to be active and space for two more was held in reserve. The septic tank had to be twenty feet or more from the house. It was a tight squeeze.

24   This gravel lane leads from the state road to our driveway. Dogwood trees in bloom lining the lane are the state flower of Virginia (and North Carolina too!).

"I wonder men dare trust themselves with other men."
                                        Shakespeare

4
The Builder
And His Bid

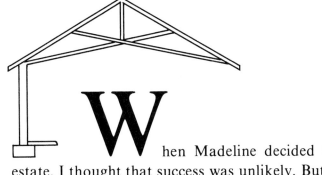

When Madeline decided that she wanted to sell real estate, I thought that success was unlikely. But she plunged in, got her state sales license, and soon sold her first house.

These days house selling usually takes place in two steps. First a house owner who wants to sell calls a real estate agent, and the agent "lists" his house for sale. A listing agent is responsible for reporting a rather detailed description of the house (room sizes, etc.), reporting the financial situation (mortage and monthly payments), helping to establish the selling price, and offering the property for sale. The information is plugged into a computer and is almost instantly made available to other real estate agents in the area. Of the thousands of agents who receive this information, the chances are that one of them will have a client who wants to buy that house. Soon step two takes place and the house is sold. Usually the office and agent that sold the house get half of the sales commission, and the office and agent who listed the house get the other half.

Then the realities of Madeline's real estate sales efforts began showing up. The phone rang. "Madeline, how would you like to list a lovely house that has a problem?" asked a friendly voice from a relocation agency. "Tell me about it," said Madeline tentatively. It should sell easily but the couple that lived there have left and the electricity has been turned off." "What's the problem?" asked Madeline. "The basement is flooded and the sump pump does not work because the electricity has been turned off. The couple are being divorced so there is no way to get either of them to cooperate on getting the problem solved. They're not talking to each other. Their lawyer says they will pay for necessary repairs; they just want the house sold. Will you take the listing?" the voice asked hopefully. Over the next few days Madeline had the basement pumped, and the furnace, air conditioner, hot water heater and sump pump (they all had been flooded) repaired and restored to working order. Yes, the grass had to be cut. Two weeks later the house was sold.

Selling other houses has involved building porches, decks, repairing termite damage, new roofs, etc. In the course of all this Madeline became acquainted with a rather talented carpenter who started off doing decks and house repairs and a few years later ended up building houses. In the beginning Madeline found him many jobs. I approached him about building our house. He would do it, but his schedule was such that he could not start our house soon. That was not acceptable to us. He did suggest, however, that we handle the subcontracts and build the house ourselves. We would save money and besides he would help by advising us.

It was a tempting offer but I decided against it. Not being familiar with the local subcontractors, I considered it impossible for me to select the reliable and hard-working ones on just a one time basis. Presumably our friend could advise us on this, but there are so very many small subcontractors involved that I would have to command a significant part of our friend's time. I suggested a fee arrangement, but he was uncomfortable with this so we droppped the approach. There is a second serious flaw with this plan. Subcontractors usually are small operators. They must of necessity look out for themselves if they are to survive in business. When a builder asks them to work on a house and they do a good job, they have the prospect of working on the builder's next house —and so on into the future. In contrast, should I ask them to bid it would be a one shot deal, and I believe I would always get second priority on my house, perhaps even the lesser skilled craftsmen. So I continued my search for a builder.

Some time ago Madeline sold a lot to a couple who wanted to build their dream house. About a year and a half later, they called and asked us to come over to the lot to see their house under construction and to discuss some things with them. I had visions of happy owners and a lead to contacting a good builder. They had a rather conventional contract with a builder but things were not going too well. The house was costing the builder more than they had expected — "but that's the builder's problem not ours." Delivery of the completed house was about five months overdue. Their biggest complaint was that "every time we make a minor change to the house the builder tries to charge us an outrageous price. We bicker back and forth and always end with some animosity and it keeps piling up." I had been through some of this with previous houses we had built; I continued the search.

After talking to other local homeowners, I found two builders who seemed reliable and capable. Both were actively building in the area, and both would take on building our house as soon as we could get plans approved by the county. Neither would take on a fixed price contract, but both gave me their written itemized estimate of the cost to build the house I had drawn. During actual building, having two bids to compare turned out to be quite valuable. Here are both estimates. When given to me, one estimate was a form filled out by hand and one was a computer printout.

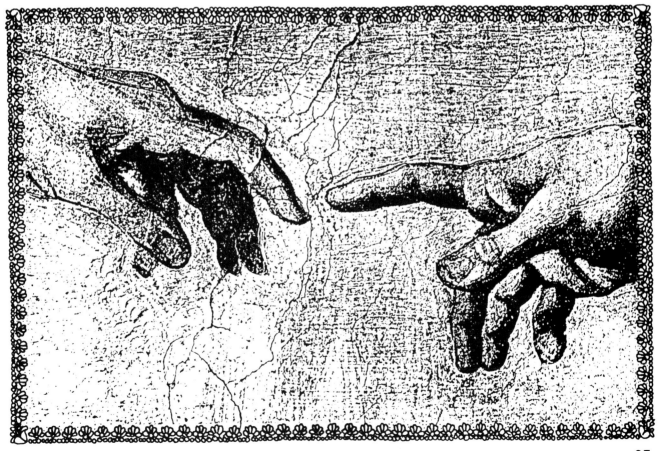

First "Builders" Cost Estimate (Wells)

ITEM	ESTIMATED COST
Site Engineering	$500
Excavate and Backfill	7,000
Trash Haul	1,000
Waterproofing/Poisoning	250
Common Labor	1,000
Gravel Under Slab	500
Permits, Fees, Temp., Elec.	500
Blueprints, Sanitation	0
Concrete	4,500
Steel	1,000
Masonry	20,000
Lumber	18,000
Trusses	5,000
Millwork	4,000
Exterior Doors and Windows	5,000
Glazing	0
Carpentry	15,000
Plumbing	10,000
Well and Septic	7,000
Heating and Air Conditioning	8,000
Electrical	5,000
Electrical Fixtures	2,000
Insulation	3,000
Roofing	6,000
Gutters and Downspouts	600
Hardware	600
Miscellaneous Tools and Supplies	500
Driveway	2,000
Flooring-Tile	3,000
Carpet	5,000
Drywall	8,000
Painting and Staining	3,000
Ceramic Tile	3,000
Weather Stripping	300
Mirrors and Bath Trim	500
Kitchen and Bath	6,000
Oil Tank	0
Supervision	16,000
Central Vac	500
Garage Doors	800
TOTAL	**$174,050**

Second "Builders" Cost Estimate

ITEM	ESTIMATED COST
Permits	$350
Surveys	600
Clearing, excavation, backfill, gravel	5,000
Concrete footings	1,500
Concrete slabs	5,000
Masonry, block and brick	16,000
Steel	1,000
Framing materials	18,000
Windows	9,000
Siding, exterior trim	4,000
Entry doors	1,500
Garage doors and openers	1,000
Interior doors and trim	5,000
Stairs and handrails	1,000
Roofing	4,000
Carpentry Labor	25,000
Plumbing	6,000
Heating	8,000
Electrical - rough in, labor	5,000
Fixtures	2,000
Insulation	3,000
Drywall	5,000
Painting	6,000
Kitchen cabinets, vanities, tops	5,000
Appliances	3,000
General floor allowance	6,000
Ceramic tile allowance	3,600
Vinyl tile - basement	1,000
Hardware - door knobs, mirrors, towel bars	1,000
Septic allowance	4,000
Well allowance	3,000
Walkway allowance	1,000
Final gravel driveway	800
Grading and seeding	1,500
Gutters and downspouts	1,200
Central vacuum	1,000
Trash removal	1,000
Landscaping allowance	1,000
Screened porch	3,000
Builder's supervisory fee	25,000
TOTAL	**$195,050**

32.5K

195
-77
122

29

I told both builders that my goal was to get the house up for $150,000. I also pointed out that missing my goal by a wide margin would simply mean not building. We were at a stage in life where major financial boo-boos could not be tolerated. The alternative would be to sell the lot and move to a less expensive area of the county, an alternative which we did not cherish.

§

The usual arrangement for financing the building of a new home is to get a "construction loan" from a local bank. Of course the owner must qualify for the loan or it's all off. The bank usually insists that the applicant not only own his lot outright but also have a sufficient down payment and adequate income to pay the loan off over the coming years. Each bank has it's own rules and policies about construction loans. By the time the house gets built, you will have spent all of the cash you put up and all of the loan money too. Then, after completion, the loan frequently is converted by the bank into a "permanent" loan on the house. The bank will not put up all of the loan money at once but resorts to what they call "draws." For example, the first draw might occur when the foundation walls have been completed and could be fifteen percent of the total loan. The second could be when the sub-flooring and rough exterior walls have been constructed and so on, until the house has been completed. Going this route with a bank entails many other restrictions. Theoretically someone from the loan office will inspect the construction at each stage before authorizing a draw. They will also require insurance to cover disasters during and after construction. Some banks collect and pay your property taxes as part of the loan terms — that way they are sure the taxes get paid. Then, in addition to county codes and covenants, the bank will have a list of its own requirements. They may require that a house be painted inside and out. I remember back when they would not allow drywall because plaster walls were required. Today drywall is in. The point I'm making is that a bank exerts a lot of influence over how you get your house up. It all costs money, and who pays for it? Your builder will be interested in your financial arrangements and can even advise you to some extent. After all, he has to put up with the restrictions too. Some of the restrictions are very good, like adequate disaster insurance. Some of the other restrictions look to me to be otherwise.

The insurance we took out for protection during construction ended up being an add-on (rider) to our existing "home owners" policy. It cost only a small amount and I have not included it in the cost of house construction.

This loan thing is a very big subject and a changing one too. It deserves a separate book and it can't be covered very well here. It's one heck of a big cost and can also be a burden in getting a house up. If you do it the way I like to do it, the loan and it's restrictions essentially go away.

I know that many hold a strong opposite view on house loans. They think it desirable to get the largest loan one can handle and this may be quite true when inflation is raging. Don't underestimate the power of persuasion and promotion by the money lenders; they are big guns and a home buyer is a small potato. Figure out your loan situation for yourself if you can and then shop about to see if you can get what *you* want. I have figured out that those who successfully use big loans on their houses to get what they want must be very smart.

Now to get on with the way we handled financing the construction of our new house. We had sold our home which was financially clear, that is, had no loans. On the day of settlement we ended up with substantial funds. These funds we quickly desposited into interest bearing accounts giving good returns but which also allowed the money to become available as needed for construction. It was an interesting exercise but again there is no good way of explaining the details here. It deserves more attention than I give it. The thrust of it all is that we were now financially ready to make an agreement with a builder to construct our house. The builders we contacted liked the arrangement of no bank involvement.

§

We picked the builder with the lowest estimate but that is not the only reason we picked him. I'm going to call him Wells although that was not his real name. Wells had built custom and speculation houses for many years; he liked owner-builder relationships and was quite philosophical about it. Wells said that years ago he had studied the pathways that led to builder-owner differences. He did not enjoy disagreements and preferred to avoid them by having an arrangement that circumvented them from the start. It's not surprising that Wells did not like hard and detailed agreements nor was he fond of voluminous house specifications. Still he recognized that the owner should get what he wants in detail.

Wells' proposition was this: the builder is actually the owner (us) and Wells is the co-builder-consultant. He would arrange for all materials, sub-contractors, licenses, permits, inspections, etc. Should we wish to use subcontractors or suppliers other than his choice, it was okay; Wells would work with them too. However, his estimate was based on those subcontractors and suppliers with whom he normally worked and knew to be reliable. In addition, since he was a builder, he could get some supplies at a builder's discount when ordered in his name. All bills would come to and be paid by us although some might come to us through Wells. Most of the subcontractors would supply us with written proposals or contracts, and if we did not like them we could negotiate for changes with or without Well's help. If we did not like or want

Wells' services, we could terminate them at any time by saying so and paying up for the week. Wells offered us a printed agreement which we could alter as we wished for his consideration. It is printed here for information but we never saw fit to use it.

MEMO OF UNDERSTANDING

This memo between _____ and Mr. Wells outlines terms under which the construction of a new house will be carried out. _____ intend to build a new house on their lot _____ of _____ in Northern, Virginia. To accomplish this they will engage the services of Mr. Wells to supervise and coordinate subcontractors and laborers as needed and to generally oversee the project including site work construction, purchasing of materials, and liaison where necessary with various state and county building officials.

Mr. Wells for his part agrees to see that the progress of the project proceeds on a timely basis, in a workmanlike manner, according to the plans and specifications, in accordance with county codes and zoning ordinances, and to adhere as strictly as possible to the proposed budget.

Mr. Wells further agrees to meet with _____ on a regular basis during the anticipated _____ weeks of construction to inform them of progress, discuss changes in the plans and specifications as such occur, to approve current expenditures for payment, forecast upcoming cash needs and discuss generally other problems and solutions.

_____ agree to pay Mr. Wells a fee for such services of $ _____ per week, paid weekly, each Tuesday.

_____ further agree: (1) to pay material suppliers and subcontractors and laborers on a timely basis according to the terms of their billing, (2) to arrange the financing of this project so that at no time will the progress of the job suffer because of lack of payment to subcontractors and suppliers (inferring both willingness and ability on the part of the _____ to spend funds for this project apart from the bank's construction loan), (3) to establish a separate checking account for construction payments and not comingle personal monies with construction funds or use construction funds for purposes other than the construction of the subject house. _____ further agree to make decisions pertaining to the decorative specifications on a timely basis so that the project will not be delayed once started.

_____   _____
        Date

What would happen if we had poor weather or an accident caused a time delay? Wells was convinced that the house could and would be finished within his time estimate, but if not, and delays were his fault, he would go ahead beyond his estimate and finish up without an additional fee. He said that no one can effectively put this down on paper so that writing about it is not worthwhile. He has a point. I was still apprehensive over one feature—there was no incentive to finish the house ahead of time. Wells' fee was $500 a week for thirty-two weeks at which time the house was to be finished. If completed ahead of time he would lose some of his fee and it seemed to me that the arrangement favored his running the time period to the very end. As you will see, that is exactly what happened. Just the same, the arrangement had some attractive features. Should the price get out of hand during construction, I could cut out some subcontracting and do selected jobs myself, such as painting, trimwork, landscaping, etc. Also I could consider handling subcontracting on my own until completion. Since I'm prone to work on my own anyway, this would not be an unsatisfactory situation for me. On the other hand, should the price get too high we would complete the house and sell it as a last resort. Finished, it would be a beautiful house in a fine location and should command a selling price well above Wells' estimate. Under the proposed arrangement we felt that we would be in control of the building process more than we had been while constructing previous homes.

I was not completely satisfied and so I probed further. Wells had completed several houses in our area and was in the process of completing more. I took time to inspect a few of them. The workmen on the job seemed to respect Wells and the structures looked good to me. One house Wells had built was right in our neighborhood. It was an attractive home from the outside; we went to the front door, rang the bell and the husband and wife appeared. They looked faintly familiar and it surfaced in our conversation that they had come through our old house when we had it for sale. They had decided to build rather than to buy. Their home was huge compared to what we wanted but it was finished reasonably well. They had a few complicated areas such as a large expensive kitchen, unusual cabinetry and a sunken recreation room. How were Wells' time estimates? Resonably good but not perfect. They had moved in with some things still to be completed. However, Wells had suggested some changes during construction which saved quite a bit of money. With the money saved, they had the house finished in the more expensive all brick exterior instead of the part brick - part wood they had originally planned. What about Wells' cost estimates — were they reasonably accurate? All of the big items were quite good but some of the smaller custom items were out of line. Since their concept of custom items was different from Wells', this might have been anticipated, but it wasn't. Were they comfortable with him, that is, did they feel he had been dishonest or shady in any way? They gave him a clean bill of health — no twinge of dishonesty anywhere. They felt Wells was financially responsible and trustworthy and they would recommend him for building our home. Driving home that evening I asked Madeline what she thought. "Hope we haven't missed anything," she said, "but it looks all right to me." It was time to shake Wells' hand and get the show on the road.

Flag day

5

Day by Day, Month by Month

The Month of March

At last we went over our informal agreement with Wells and shook hands. Up until this point our dream house had been just that — a dream whose only brush with reality was a two dimensional set of house plans. Now, after years of preparation, the task of putting our dreams into the reality of brick and mortar was underway. My first encounter with this reality occurred when the builder informed me that a jungle of information was needed before the bulldozer could dig up its first scoop of dirt. At least ten copies of the house plans were necessary for the many subcontractors' bids and permits. A variety of county offices, including the health and structures departments, had to give approval. Plans pass from one county office to the next in sequence, and it *just takes time*. In addition, other arrangements such as temporary electrical power had to be approved. Wells cautioned us that perhaps two months would pass before much building action could take place. Keeping in mind that the builder was being paid $500 a week, one can get a little antsy writing a log of no activity day after day.

Before actual construction got underway, I asked Wells to pinpoint several items on his cost estimates where he thought they might be reduced. However, he was not confident this could be achieved. For example, I estimated that because of the side loading garage, we would need a total of about 1,000 cubic yards of fill dirt. This concerned me because providing this amount of dirt could be quite costly. I was pleased when Wells said he thought he had located some free fill dirt. He asked that I open up the fence where the final driveway entrance would be and mark the boundaries for the fill. He could pay some men to do it, but I elected to save the money and do it myself. In a small way the informal agreement with Wells had started to work. During this period I arranged with the electric power company, VEPCO, for temporary power. Also, the gas company said that we were approved for gas, and they would install the two hundred foot gas line from the county highway to the house at no cost. Since we were the builders and the owners, it was appropriate that we undertook these arrangements with the gas and electric power company, although Wells would have done it had I asked him to.

March, day by day

March 13 • After several previous planning meetings we met with Wells and requested that he start work on our new house. He agreed to do so and asked that I make some minor changes to the house plans and furnish him ten copies. At an earlier meeting I had asked him if his cost estimate could be reduced. He pointed to several items and gave a maximum reduction of $12,600 but said he was not optimistic about this.

• Confirmed that I was to pay Wells $500 a week for 32 weeks, a total of $16,000. Should the time overrun, barring unusual circumstances, he would finish the house but not require additional payment beyond the 32 weeks. He would let me know when first payment was due.

March 14 • Made the minor house plan changes which Wells had requested and had ten copies printed and delivered to him.

• Wells had been in touch with a registered surveyor to stake out the official house location on the lot. If the county considers ours to be a corner lot there may be complications on house to road set-back dimensions. He will try to resolve.

- Wells thought that he had located some free fill dirt, and requested that I open the fence where the final driveway would enter and mark boundaries where fill dirt should be dumped.

March 15
- Opened the fence large enough for trucks to enter and located dirt fill boundaries.

March 16
- NA (No Activity)

March 17
- Sunday. Put up direction signs for dump trucks and put string around boundaries for dumping.
- Checked and confirmed my rough location stakes for the house and the elevation for the basement floor in case this would help the surveyor.

March 18
- Wells said that I should get in touch with the Virginia Power Company (VEPCO) to request authorization for temporary power at the building site.

March 19
- Called VEPCO. They needed a letter from me requesting both temporary and permanent electric power along with a $166 application fee. I typed and sent it.
- Washington Gas Light called (I had contacted them earlier about gas) and said that they will install a gas line to the new house at no charge. They will run the line from the county highway to the house gas meter (about 200 feet). I will pay for installation of pipe inside the house to gas furnace.
- Vepco said that nearest transformers to my house (for temporary power) were located at a distance on Mr. G's property. For my own protection they suggested I get a written note from him agreeing to the hookup.

March 20
- NA

March 21
- Found the nearest transformer to be on a lot about 300 feet away. Found Mr. G who furnished a typed signed note giving his okay to make the temporary hook-up on his property.

March 22
- Received VEPCO okay for temporary power hook-up. I sent a copy to Wells.

March 23
- NA

March 24
- Sunday. NA

March 25
- NA

March 26
- NA

March 27
- NA

March 28
- NA

March 29
- NA

March 30
- NA

March 31
- Sunday. Called Wells and made date to drive to county seat to get plan approvals started.

The Month of April

On April Fool's day Wells and I went to the county seat and made application for a building permit. We submitted the house plans in the number they needed; I paid for the building permit, the well permit, and the environmental conservation permit and hoped that we had made all the necessary arrangements to satisfy the county. The operation is such that one can't be sure. Later in the month, Wells was back in touch with the county and reported that the health office had cleared the septic tank, drain field and house plans. They were now in the final stages of approval for the building permit.

I went to the lot and found that some of the preliminary work was underway. The electrician had installed equipment at the transformer but had not yet run wires to the house. The surveyor had staked out the house position on the lot, which matched my rough layout quite well. Wells was ready to order a bulldozer to dig the basement but decided not to proceed until final county approval had been given. Finally Wells informed me that he had the building permit in hand and that he would have the bulldozer digging the basement the next day. Twenty-four hours later, the bulldozer finished its work. At day's end the operator and I were the only two there so I signed his work sheet showing 8½ hours work time.

Several days of inactivity passed before Wells called again. He and his family had been in an accident. Wells had a badly sprained leg and other members of his family had been hurt, one seriously. I sympathized with Wells' situation but, of course, I wondered what this would do to our building schedule which seemed slow to me already. Although walking was severely curtailed, Wells showed up four days after the accident and directed the excavation for the footings. A backhoe cut the rough footings into the ground and then Bill, the mason, and his crew accomplished the finishing touches by hand shoveling. Wells explained that he previously had so many complaints from Bill about uneven footings that he had asked Bill to take on the job himself — fewer complaints that way.

The county inspector was scheduled to approve the footing excavations in the morning, so Wells had ordered the concrete for the footings to be delivered early in the afternoon. A crew to place and finish the concrete was already waiting to do the job when the inspector arrived. It was obvious that he was quite upset. There was no sign at the driveway entrance to indicate our lot and so he wasted twenty minutes looking for us. He made a pass around the footings and stated that he would not approve them — too many soft spots. We explained that there was concrete coming and we would do as he directed to meet his approval — he drove off without further conversation. Wells then drove to a commercial engineering office and came back with their inspector. The county recognizes approvals by such licensed engineers. He had a ground probe device which he thrust into the earth at close intervals (builders call it a magic wand). Dig here a little, there a little, then test again. Okay, it's approved! The concrete truck had been sitting there joyously grinding away. At last it belched forth its innards and we had footings.

April, day by day

April 1 • Wells and I went to county seat and submitted house plans for their many approvals. We also applied for a building permit.

April 2 • NA (No Activity)

April 3 • NA

April 4 • NA

April 5 • NA

April 6 • Electrician installed temporary station at transformer but had not run wires to house.

April 7 • Sunday. NA

April 8 • NA

April 9 • NA

April 10 • NA

April 11 • Wells went to county seat. The health office had cleared the house plans and they were now in the final stages of approval for building permit. He paid $97 permit fee and passed receipt to me so I could pay him, which I did.

April 12 • NA

April 13 • NA

April 14 • Sunday. NA

April 15 • Drove to county seat and paid $1,000 environmental conservation bond. This is to be returned to us upon satisfactory completion of house grounds (97% of bare areas covered with grass).

     • Told Wells that surveyors had not yet staked out the house on the lot.

April 16 • NA

April 17 • NA

April 18 • NA

April 19 • Wells picked up building permit at county seat.

April 20 • Surveyors staked out house position.

April 21 • Sunday. NA

April 22 • Bulldozer excavated basement.
April 23 • NA
April 24 • NA
April 25 • Wells called. He had been in an accident and had a badly sprained leg. Members of his family were hurt, one seriously.
April 26 • NA
April 27 • NA
April 28 • Sunday. Wells called to say footings would be excavated tomorrow.
April 29 • Footings were excavated by backhoe. The mason and his crew finished by hand shoveling.
April 30 • Completed hand trimming of footings.
• County inspector showed but would not approve footings because of softness in garage area. He was upset because I had not placed a house number sign at road entrance and he had lost time finding us. He drove off before we could satisfy him. Wells found a county certified engineer who, with his magic wand, had us dig out some soft spots. He then approved. The concrete arrived, was poured, and footings were completed late in the day.

The Month of May

When drawing the house plans, I had selected a well-known and expensive brand of wooden windows. Not only were they of high quality but the rough opening dimensions for them were readily available, and so I used that information to get the house plans done. Now Wells was telling me that I could save $3,000 or more if I were willing to switch to a new "space age" aluminum Noranda window. These windows are made of an inner and outer shell. The two shells are pieced together with a "thermal barrier" (insulating adhesive) which overcomes much of the objections to earlier metal window designs. The old designs conducted too much heat into the house in summer and out of the house in winter. The old designs also sweat a lot in the winter. Madeline and I went to see these new windows installed in a house Wells had under construction. We found their appearance to be satisfactory and therefore decided to go with the Noranda windows. Wells gave me a copy of the technical information needed and I revised the house plans to incorporate the new windows. Having now lived in the house through the winter, we find them to be quite good — very airtight and little or no sweating. There are undoubtedly other brands that compete but we selected Noranda because Wells recommended them, the carpenter already knew how to install them, and besides, the price was right.

At Wells' suggestion we elected to use Noranda aluminum windows. These are constructed of an inner and outer shell joined together by a thermal adhesive barrier which resists heat loss and interior sweating.

Madeline and I drove to the major brick supplier in the area and picked out the brick for the house. We selected General Shale S/S Flashed Patina 2911-420, which Wells said was "pretty jazzy." They had 27,000 in stock and Wells' rough estimate for our house was 10,000, so there would be no delay in getting the brick we wanted.

I had specified a Heatilator (warm-air circulating) fireplace and had drawn plans to accommodate their 36 inch model. Bill, the mason, said he would install it but preferred a brand called Heatform because he was familiar with the Heatform installation. I counted that as a plus — fewer chances for mistakes. I obtained information on their 36 inch model from a local Heatform dealer. It fit within the dimensions of the chimney, so I told Wells to proceed with the Heatform fireplace. The cost would be included in the mason's quotation. A feature in our plans is worth mentioning here. Air circulating fireplaces are usually installed with a raised hearth in which air intake grills are located in the face of the hearth. This draws cool air from the floor, heats it, and exhausts it into the room above the fireplace. I remember sitting on such a hearth once and getting cold feet from the incoming air. By lowering the air intake grills about two feet and pulling air from the basement ceiling area, I avoided the draft on the floor and also much of the upstairs fan noise (fans are located at the air intake grills). In the summer, I save a little on air conditioning costs by running the fireplace fans to draw the cool basement air to the upstairs.

...ad decided not to have a garden the year we built the house, ...e garden area, tilled it and ended up planting it in Silver Queen ...st year gardens are poor but corn is a rugged crop. It turned out to ...a decision because we had a great corn crop with practically no ...on to the garden. We gave corn to Wells, Bill, Binney the carpenter, and ...d our freezer besides. While I was tilling, the concrete block for the ...oundation walls arrived and the next day Bill and his crew came to put them up. Bill needed water for mortar and we had not dug our well yet. Could he run a hose from the house over there? "I'll investigate," I said, and went over to size up the situation. To my surprise, my new neighbor had moved in just that day! Yes, I could draw water from their outside hose faucets. And yes, I gave them some Silver Queen corn too.

Before leaving on a trip to Florida to visit my family for a week, Wells and I drove to a supplier that specialized in metal building products. We ordered several outside metal doors and the small steel truss beams (joists) that would support the concrete floor for the screened porch. I wanted to know from Wells if there was business I should attend to before leaving. He said I should pay $400 to the backhoe operator who dug the footings. Also, I should pay the bill for the concrete (which had been sent to Wells since he had ordered it). In addition, I should make a check for $5,000 to Bill for masonry work and leave it with Wells. Wells would give the check to Bill when he completed the foundation walls. I let Wells know that I did not like the arrangement with Bill. I felt he should give me a quotation for the whole job and I should approve the quotation before I pay him. Wells promised to get an estimate, but my not being there the next week could complicate things, since by the the time we returned, the masons would have finished enough work for their first draw. I had to leave the check with Wells.

When we returned, I was pleased to find that the basement/foundation walls were complete. Before long, the steel beams to support the floor as well as wood for the floor joists had arrived. Wells told me that the county had approved the house for 2 x 10 inch floor joists but I had specified 2 x 12 inch joists. Did I want the 2 x 10's? It would save money. It's just one of those peculiarities about houses — joists can have ample strength but still be too flexible, jouncy and shakey. Sometimes you feel it when you walk by a table and see the flowers in a vase sway a little, or maybe a lot! No, the floor is not about to fall through but the jouncing is a bit much. Now, 2 x 12's are much stiffer than 2 x 10's and yes, I did want them. So it was that a load of 2 x 12's showed up at the lot along with a load of plywood for the subflooring. The next day, tons of gravel were dumped near the basement door to be spread over the basement floor.

During the month of May, I reviewed with Wells the nature of the four main subcontracts on the house: masonry, carpentry, lumber and plumbing. I wanted to understand how things would work. According to Wells, the mason's subcontract would be quite different from the carpenter's contract. Bill's contract for masonry would include all materials and labor. It was a good way of handling all of the special materials he needed like various sizes of concrete blocks, masonry, and steel lintels to span over the top of windows and door openings. He needed steel reinforcement mesh between every other block course and various kinds of brick, some solid for paving the hearth and front entranceway, and some hollow. It would be difficult for someone not in the trade to order the proper kinds and amounts of supplies he needed. The only thing I furnished for him was the water. I liked the way the mason's contract was set up, however, I was still a bit uneasy since I had no written bid from Bill as yet, and he had already been paid his first draw. In contrast, the carpenter would supply all labor and small attachment fittings such as various types of nails, glue, plywood clips, etc., but the lumber and millwork were furnished separately. Wells therefore asked me to open an account at the local lumber and millwork firm (lumberyard). It was a credit account in my name and I had to go through setting that up. Keep in mind that all bills were paid by me, even though some were sent through the builder. During the month of May, Wells also handed me a copy of a proposed contract for the plumbing and asked that I review it and make changes with the plumber if necessary. Speaking of plumbing, it was time to get a county inspector out to give his blessing on the proposed septic tank, well, and drain field location. I called and made the arrangements. And so by the end of May, I had a better understanding of how the major subcontracts on the house would work. In many ways they were similar, yet each had to be tailored to fit the needs and personalities of the individual subcontractors.

Binny, the head carpenter, and his crew went to work with amazing energy although they frequently ran out of supplies which had to be ordered from the lumberyard. Within a couple of days they had the floor joists up and steel beams in place. One of the steel beams was bent and had a curve of about eight inches. They put some jacks on it and the beam gave up its curve to conform to a straight line, much to my relief.

The carpentry contract showed up in our mail. Again, I had the advantage of having two builders' estimates to check against. It was a little higher than Wells' estimate but substantially less than the second builder's estimate. Wells said it was a good bid and it appeared competitive so I signed it. The carpenters had started work before I had a signed contract and that made me uncomfortable. No payments were made though until the contract was signed, so I was less upset over this than I was with the mason's contract.

43

...one Spring morning at the lot and was greeted with a call of ...Binney, his business partner brother, and the carpentry crew ...ing me. The brother spoke: "Charlie, we need a shittery or you're ...y to get it in your basement!" "Okay, I'll look into it," I said. Portable ...un sixty dollars a month and they deliver, service and remove them as ...ested. I rented one and, I guess, made the carpenters happier.

The carpenters asked for it.

May, day by day

May 1   •   NA (No Activity)

May 2   •   Wells took us to a house he was building and showed us the Noranda windows he recommended. We agreed to use them in our house. I asked Wells to get me a brochure giving window dimensions.

     •   Went to a local brick supplier and selected the brick for the house. Checked their stock and they had about twice as many as we needed.

     •   Drove to a local Heatform fireplace distributor and obtained information on sizes of their products.

May 3   •   Gave Wells information on our brick selection and also told him to go ahead with 36 inch Heatform fireplace. Wells would relay this information to Bill.

May 4 • Wells said the concrete block for foundation walls would arrive Monday.

• Wells informed me he would leave a six-foot wide opening to the ground at one of the basement windows so that a Bobcat (small bulldozer-type machine) could later get into the basement to spread gravel.

May 5 • Sunday. Plowed the garden and planted corn.

May 6 • Concrete block arrived.

May 7 • Bill and crew arrived and started laying concrete blocks.

May 8 • Wells and I drove to a firm in Maryland which specializes in metal construction products. Ordered exterior steel doors for garage and basement entrances. Ordered the steel trusses (joists) to support the concrete floor for the screened porch.

• Wells and I delivered the metal door frames to the lot so Bill could set them into the foundation walls.

May 9 • Wells gave me the information brochure on the Noranda windows and I prepared a new window schedule to suit.

May 10 • Gave copies of new window schedule to Wells. In laying the foundation walls, Bill would use the rough openings on the window schedule and the windows would be fit into these later.

• Told Wells I was going to Florida for a week. He requested that I send $400 to the backhoe operator for excavating the footings, and pay the bill for the concrete. While I was gone, Bill would finish the foundation walls and would want his first draw. I should leave a check with Wells for $5,000 to be given to Bill when he finished. I told Wells that I did not like it because I still had not received a bid from Bill. Wells agreed and said he would ask Bill for a bid in writing. Left the check with Wells, made out to Bill.

May 11 • NA

May 12 • Sunday through May 16. Trip to Florida.

May 17 • Foundation walls finished.

• Wells ordered steel beams to support the floor and gravel for the basement. Too much rain and mud for trucks to deliver the gravel.

May 18 • NA

May 19 • Sunday. NA

May 20 • Plywood for subfloor and wood floor joists delivered to lot.

May 21	• Carpenters arrived and put up as much of the floor joists as they could. They needed steel beams but these had not been delivered yet.
	• Gravel for basement floor delivered.
	• Masonry crew removed their scaffolding.
May 22	• Gravel was placed into basement and leveled by Bobcat.
	• Steel beams and columns arrived followed by carpenters who installed them. More plywood is needed to finish the sub-flooring.
	• Called the firm supplying the porch floor steel trusses and found them waiting for word on the exact length. I measured the span on the foundation walls and called them back with dimensions.
	• Wells asked me to establish a credit account in my name with the lumberyard.
May 23	• The steel beam which the carpenters had erected had an eight inch warp in it. I asked Wells to look into it.
May 24	• Using jacks, the carpenters straightened the warp in the steel beam. Carpenters continued to install the subflooring but again ran out of plywood. More plywood arrived just at quitting time.
May 25	• Carpenters completed the floor joists and subfloor.
May 26	• Sunday. NA
May 27	• Memorial Day. NA
May 28	• Binney sent me a written quote for the carpentry labor. It was not entirely definitive and I was more satisfied after he explained the work that it covered.
	• Binney asked that a portable toilet be placed on the lot. I called a couple of places and made arrangements with one of them.
May 29	• Showed the carpentry contract to Wells who said it was a good price. Compared Binny's bid of $16,454 to Well's original estimate of $15,000. It looked okay so I signed it. Asked Wells if I were to furnish the Heatform fireplace or was Bill to furnish it as part of his contract. Bill would furnish.
	• Told Wells I still had no bid from Bill and that I did not like it because he had already done so much work and had been paid his first draw.
	• Carpenters erected most of the exterior and interior walls.
	• Wells gave me a copy of the proposed plumbing contract and suggested I get in touch with the plumber, to iron out any changes I might want.

May 30 • Carpenters still working erecting walls.
        • Met with representative of the Gas company and all was as he expected. They will not install the gas line to the house until after final grading.
May 31 • NA

Once the subflooring has been installed it is advisable to get the house under roof as soon as possible. The subflooring is level and does not shed water very well. Unless protected by the roof, it will soon start to deteriorate. Rough subflooring and floor squeeks can result.

The Month of June

Wells started off the month of June with a suprise announcement — the roof trusses would not be delivered for two or three weeks! The trusses had been ordered weeks ago, and I was not expecting this delay. The exterior walls were all but complete, and the carpenters were ready and waiting for the trusses. More important than the simple delay was the fact that we would not get under roof right away, and the walls and plywood subfloor would have to withstand the ravages of the weather during the interim. Wood changes shape when exposed to the weather. Walls, though built true, begin to change dimensions and plywood subflooring starts to deteriorate and de-laminate. It looked like we would have to hope for good weather and put up with the delay.

I made arrangements to meet the plumber, Greenie, at the site to go over the plumbing requirements with him. His proposed contract did not reflect all the features I wanted so I asked him to modify it. A few days later he presented the revised contract which I thought was too high in price. Greenie explained that the standard tub for the hall bath was about average in cost, but that the platform tub and fixtures which I had selected for the master bathroom were high-priced items. The tub was about $1,400 and the faucet itself was over $700. After we revised the contract to allow a fixed amount of $1,500 for the tub and faucet combined, I signed it. Greenie wanted me to move a wall which butted against the end of the tub so that a less expensive tub would fit. I did not like the tub he proposed so I decided to see what I could find on my own. I went to a plumbing supply house and eventually found one that I thought was satisfactory — and it beat the $1,500 allowance! Later I discovered that I could get the tub and fixtures at an even lower price through the kitchen cabinet supplier we selected, provided that we buy our kitchen cabinets there. I presented the price for the tub and fixtures to Greenie and he could not beat it. I know that Greenie wanted to furnish the tub and fixtures but his price was about $250 over mine, so tongue in cheek, I told him I would supply them. Greenie did not seem to enjoy this little episode. Later, Greenie told me where he wanted the water line and gas pipe to enter the basement walls. Should the water line and gas pipe enter at a different place, it would cause him some extra cost. Later, this came up again. By the end of the month, Greenie had installed all under-the-basement-floor plumbing and had started the plumbing at the first floor level.

In the second week of June, Wells handed me a copy of the proposed masonry contract. It was $5,723 over Wells' original estimate of $20,000 and $9,723 over the estimate of the second builders bid! I found this upsetting, especially since I had already (at Wells' request) made an initial payment on the first draw, and we were pretty well locked in. I asked Wells to contact Bill and try to get a reduction in price. When Bill did not respond, I called him myself and gave him my figures. He said he would reconsider his quote and let me know.

Madeline had a pretty good idea of what she wanted in kitchen cabinets, counter tops, sinks, and appliances. We took a couple of days and just bounced around the various local suppliers to get ourselves acquainted with what was available. Wells suggested one kitchen shop that had Canadian-made cabinets he thought were good quality for less cost. Eventually we settled on Wells' suggestion of the Canadian cabinets, and we also took advantage of the discount prices they offered on kitchen appliances. The next step was to measure the kitchen walls (they are always a little different from the plans) and give the information to the kitchen people. In turn, they made an exact layout of the cabinets, work surfaces, etc. After reviewing the plans, they pointed out that having the refrigerator so close to the "L" corner of the work surface would cut down on convenient kitchen operation. So I took their advice and moved the walls a bit on the plans in order to achieve the clearance they recommended. I gave the wall changes to both the carpenter and kitchen suppliers and the problem was solved. Next I asked a second kitchen supply shop to give us a bid on the cabinets and I compared this to the first bid. It confirmed that the first bid was a lower price and so I signed with them. As it happened this supplier also furnished the platform bathtub at a price lower than the plumber quoted.

Two men and a tank truck arrived and sprayed a coating of black asphalt over the outside foundation walls where cement parging had been applied. They came, sprayed, and departed so fast that I almost missed them. The bill was suprisingly low at $100 which I promptly paid. This was a low overhead job with no contract, just a call from Wells and an on-the-site payment.

Toward the middle of the month, a county inspector arrived and established the exact location for the well, septic tank and drain field.

It was time to pick out the roof shingles. Madeline and I went to several shingle suppliers, but they had only a limited selection. We finally visited the one Wells recommended, which was some distance away, but at least they did have quite a few shingles to choose from. We took along both brick and wood siding samples for color matching. Eventually we selected Certainteed brand "Weatherblind" Sealdon 225 pounds per square with a 20 year warranty and I gave this information to Wells for transmittal to the roofers.

It was also time to select the tile for the bathrooms and front entrance hall. In a meeting with Brownie, the tile contractor, I explained the job and left a set of plans with him. He promised to stop by the house and subsequently send us a proposal. We then went to the display store where Brownie bought his tile, and examined our various choices. After all that, Madeline settled on plain 4 x 4 inch white tile for both baths and a tan 10 x 10 inch tile for the entrance hall.

Leveling of the gravel in the basement was done with a Bobcat and later refined by hand shoveling and raking. Reinforcing steel mesh (furnished by the concrete finisher) was then placed on top of the gravel. Then came the concrete gushing through the basement windows. It was raked into place and finished by hand at the price of fifty cents per square foot plus a couple of extras for step-openings at exterior doors. The total came to $1,200. Neither of the builders' cost estimates showed this figure separately so I had no basis for judging it. Here, there was no contract with the concrete finisher, just a bill for the job. Wells thought the price to be reasonable so I paid it.

The Bobcat is like a mini-bulldozer and is a very useful machine. Much less expensive to rent than a bulldozer, it can transport gravel and dirt into tight places and then spread and level it.

The carpenters finished the framing for the interior and exterior walls, and the roof trusses finally showed up, as did the plywood to cover the trusses once they were in place. When the crane arrived, the operator rigged it with a main boom plus a mini-boom at the top end. Trusses were lifted from the pile on the ground, one at a time, and swung into place on top of the exterior walls. Each truss when lifted to height, looked like a little cob web swinging across the sky. The carpenters worked with amazing skill, agility and good nature. "Ya-hoo, send me another truss!" Once swung into place by the crane and carefully positioned by the carpenter, the trusses were spiked onto the walls and then aligned with wood strips at the peak. The work went quickly and by the end of the day the crane had folded up its booms and gone home. The carpenter crew must have been exhausted.

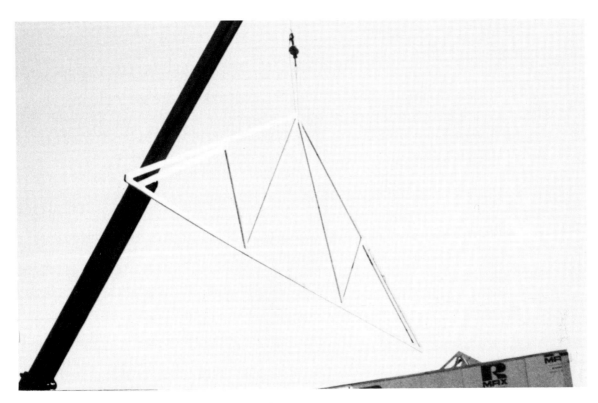

Setting roof trusses
Like cobwebs in the sky

Next came the plywood sheathing to cover the trusses. Again the carpenters worked tirelessly, and swiftly completed this job too. Binney called from the roof to one of his carpenters working in the basement. "Come on up here, Joey, I need you." Now, at this stage of construction there were no stairs in the house but Joey went straight up through the house structures and in only a few seconds was on the roof! "Okay boss, what is it?" I never ceased to be amazed at the endless energy and agility of the carpenters.

A few days later Hagen, the roofer, showed and "papered" the plywood roof sheathing with tarred roofing felt. It was none too soon because the plywood sub-flooring had started to de-laminate in spots where the rain water had not drained well.

We still had no temporary power. Although the electrician had run a wire from the transformer to the house, the wire was faulty. The carpenters, in order not to be held up, rented a gasoline powered generator and ran their saws and other electrically powered tools from this. On the bill for their first draw, I noticed that Binney had added a separate extra charge to cover this. It ended up that I paid for the temporary electrical service and the generator too. I decided not to fuss about it and be grateful that we avoided another delay. The electrician, Demper, replaced the original wire with a new one and for a little while it worked. One day the carpenters' electric saws started to jerk on and off. There was a big flash followed by smoke at the transformer connection and then no power at all. "Can't work without power," said Binney, "we'll have to leave." "Hold on a moment," I said, "can you work off an extension cord from my neighbor's house?" "I guess so," replied Binney. So once again I went to my new neighbor's house. The last time was to draw water, this time it was to draw electric power. "Would you mind?" I asked. "It would help us out of a jam and I'd be glad to pay for it. If so, it would only be for a day or two — until I get my line fixed." My neighbor was most co-operative. "It will be all right and don't worry about paying for it," he said. So I returned to the lot and told Binney. "It's okay to run the extension cord; the plug is on the deck wall."

All the windows for the house showed up in one large truck. The driver said he could not deliver them until payment was made and I gave him a check on the spot. There were no other workmen about so the driver and I unloaded the windows from the truck into the basement on one of the hottest days of the summer.

June, day by day

June 1 • Caught Wells on the lot and he said that roof trusses would not be delivered for two or three weeks!

• Carpenters said that the walls for the garage were being nailed together. Because of the rough ground around that part of the house, however, they would await a crane to place the roof trusses and the garage walls.

June 2 • Sunday. NA (No Activity)

June 3 • NA

June 4 • NA

June 5 • Met with Wells and the plumber, Greenie, and went over plumbing work for the house. I had a number of changes to what Greenie recommended. He had a proposed contract with him but I asked him to revise it.

• Wells handed me a proposed contract for the masonry. It was $5,723 over Wells' estimate so I asked Wells to go back to Bill and try for a lower bid. I felt that contract proposals on such major cost items should have been settled before we got to this stage of building.

52

June 6 • Bill worked on the brickwork for the front entrance. He said that he needed money and I offered to pay the next draw of his contract, which was due, even though I was not in agreement with his proposed contract. I gave him a check for the draw.

• Madeline and I spent the rest of the day looking at displays of kitchen and bath cabinets, sinks and roof shingles.

June 7 • Called Wells and told him to talk to Bill in an effort to reduce the price on the proposed masonry contract. Madeline and I went to a kitchen supplier and discussed our kitchen plans. Their prices were good and they had Canadian-made cabinets which Wells recommended.

• Went back to the house and made measurements of the walls and working spaces in the kitchen. Took them to the kitchen supplier and they made up a detailed layout to the actual dimensions. They pointed out that the refrigerator door was cramping its corner space so I revised the layout slightly and solved the problem.

June 8 • NA

June 9 • Sunday. NA

June 10 • Made a new drawing of the kitchen layout and had copies made. Took one copy to the kitchen supplier so they could make up a formal bid. They called back that evening and gave an estimate which sounded reasonable. Also drove by the plumbing shop and picked up Greenie's new proposed plumbing contract. It looked a little high in price.

June 11 • The county inspector arrived and established the exact location for the well, septic tank, and drain field.

• Met with Greenie and asked why his contract price was so high. He said that the tub and faucet I had chosen were high-priced . I did not like his proposed alternate but I asked him to reprice the contract and to include a specific allowance for the tub and faucet. The allowance he recommended was $1,500 which we accepted. Went to a second kitchen supplier and asked for a price on the cabinets according to my revised plan.

June 12 • Visited two plumbing supply houses and found a couple of tubs and faucets which were under the $1,500 allowance.

June 13 • The plywood for the roof sheathing was delivered to the lot.

• The plumber completed his work on the pipes which go under the basement floor concrete slab.

June 14 • Carpenters working in preparation for roof trusses. I gave Binney a copy of the new kitchen plan with minor wall change to accommodate the new position for the refrigerator.

• Picked up the second bid on kitchen cabinets and found it to be higher than the first one. I decided to go with the first bid, which included the Canadian cabinets. Madeline and I visited a kitchen appliance discount house. A gas stove with all the features we wanted was not available, so eventually we found an electric stove which was satisfactory.

June 15 • The actual bathroom dimensions turned out to be about six inches longer than the plan called for. I found that the carpenter had used a standard hall width for the "L" section at the end of the main hall. My house plans called for a hall width six inches wider than the standard width. Binney would change it if I insisted but after I checked it over and everything in the hall such as door openings seemed to function all right, I told him to leave it, although it would have been better as planned.

• The new tub selection fit easily into the slightly larger bathroom dimensions which resulted from the narrower hall. I made up a new drawing showing the actual dimensions and gave a copy to Greenie and the tile contractor.

• There was a good sale on the masonry waterproof paint I planned to use (on the outside wall on the back of the house) so I bought enough to do the entire job. I planned to paint this myself so the paint would have to be stored a few months until I could get around to painting.

June 16 • Sunday. Madeline and I spent the day evaluating kitchen appliances in various showrooms.

June 17 • Gravel was transported from the yard into the basement using a Bobcat and then leveled in preparation for concrete.

• Signed contract for Canadian-made kitchen cabinets.

June 18 • Carpenters set roof trusses — a big job and a dangerous one.

• The kitchen supplier who will furnish our kitchen cabinets will also furnish appliances, some sinks, and other plumbing items at wholesale prices. I asked them about the bathtub and faucet and they gave me the best price I had seen.

June 19 • Met with Greenie and gave him the prices I had obtained for the tub and faucet. I asked him to meet or better them.

- Met with tile contractor, Brownie, which Wells had recommended and gave him a copy of the house plans so he could give us a bid. He sent us to a showroom where we could make a choice of tiles. After comparisons, Madeline decided on white 4x4 inch tile for both baths and 10x10 inch tan tile for the front entrance foyer.
- At the house the concrete for the basement had already been poured and finished by the time I got there.
- Carpenters were putting on the roof sheathing.
- Still no temporary power at the house. The carpenters have been using a portable electric generator and the bill for their second draw shows an added charge for renting it.

June 20
- Told Wells we had made final selections on the roof shingles. He said he would pass this information on to his recommended roofing contractor, Hagen, and get me a price quote.
- Wells said that the county requires a drain set in gravel to be placed around the footings. I told him that I had the time to do it myself and not to hire someone.
- Bill had not responded to Wells' request for re-evaluating his price bid on the masonry work. So I called Bill myself and explained why I thought his bid was too high. He said he would go over it and get back to me.

June 21
- Worked on drain around footings.

June 22
- Completed drain around footings.

June 23
- Sunday. NA

June 24
- Wells said that a driver with a truckload of windows was at the house. It was a C.O.D. order and I should take a check for $4,896 to the driver. When I got there I found one sinewy but small man and a big truckload of windows. Each window was in a huge cardboard box. He asked if there were any workmen around to unload, and as luck would have it, there weren't any. Rather than turn him away I offered to help him unload. So on a beastly hot and humid afternoon, he and I unloaded the truck and stashed the windows in the basement.

June 25
- The extra plywood to complete the roof sheathing was delivered. We were still not completely under roof and I noticed some delaminating of the plywood subflooring from rain and weather — a disappointing and frustrating situation.

June 26 • Carpenters finished roof sheathing but found temporary electric power going on and off. Then suddenly, a smoky flash at the transformer box, and the electricity was off for good. I went to my neighbor and asked if we could plug into their outside outlet until we could get our wires fixed and he said okay. Wells promised to check into getting our temporary electric power fixed.

• Carpenters placed windows at various wall openings in preparation for installation.

June 27 • Greenie called and said that his bid for the tub and faucet was $1,207. This compared to a $957 quote from our kitchen supplier. So I told Greenie that we would furnish these items separately. Actually I wanted him to furnish them but decided that the $250 difference was worth the risk of his being upset over it, or of us chipping the tub before it got into his hands.

June 28 • Plumbers almost completed installation of drain pipes in first floor level.

• Carpenters had trouble assembling and installing windows. Only two windows installed today.

• Called Bill again about reducing price on masonry work but he had not reviewed it. He promised to do it over the weekend.

June 29 • At last Hagen, the roofer, and his crew papered the roof.

June 30 • Sunday. NA

The Month of July

One day early in July, the bath tub for the master bathroom arrived while the plumbers happened to be installing pipes. Greenie was a little annoyed since he had not intended to wrestle the tub from the truck into the house, and the truck driver was the only person who arrived with it. "How in the hell ya gonna get it into the house with this little scrawny driver?" asked Greenie. "Ya know if this thing gets chipped, it's not my fault 'till it's in the bathroom." Finally Greenie called his two sons who were working with him, and asked them to unload the tub and get it into the house. It was not new work for them, still it was all they could handle just to slide the crated tub out of the truck. Then they had to put it on boards, slide it across the yard, up the steps, down the hall, and finally into the bathroom.

We had decided to have a big family get-together at the beach during the second week of July. While away, I kept in touch with Wells by phone. During this time, the house was to be backfilled, that is, dirt which had been removed so that the foundation walls could be built would be pushed back into place against the outside of the foundation walls. This brings the earth against the outside of the house to its final level. Before this is done, however, the foundation walls and the drain pipe installed on top of the footings had to be approved by a county inspector. When we got back from the beach, this work was completed and for the first time I could envision how the house would look when finished.

While away I also called Bill and asked if he had completed the review of his bid on the masonry work. He had not and it took a couple more calls before he gave me an answer. He finally condescended to reduce the price from $25,723 to $24,000. I still thought that the $24,000 was high but I accepted it as probably the best I could do under the circumstances.

The location for all light switches, wall plugs, and other electrical conveniences can be indicated on the house plans. There are standard symbols for these things and I did include them when drawing up plans for previous homes. Envisioning the best locations for electrical items from a set of house plans, however, is an imperfect endeavor. It always ends up the same anyway —you go through the incomplete house with the electrician and simply mark the floor, ceiling or frame, where you want each item to be placed. Planning, of course, is very worthwhile, but I find it best to do this when the walls are up and one can actually see the distances and space relationships. So I spent a couple of days with Madeline going through the house and deciding the location of electrical items. Then when the electrician showed up I went through the house again with him marking things the way we wanted them. During the installation of the wiring, Demper told me he could install an automatic exhaust fan for $150. I told him to go ahead and put it in, and I'd give him a check separate from his contract. That's all there was to it. By the end of the month, the wiring for the house was essentially completed.

There are people who specialize in furnishing stairs, and it's a good thing too. Stairs are a tricky business to get right, and there are also local codes about stairs and stairwells which are not always self-evident. Wells arranged a meeting at the house with the "stair-man." He asked a few pertinent questions to which I answered, "No, they would be covered with carpet. The wood on the sides would be painted so there would be no need for expensive woods in the staircase." The "stair-man" took some measurements, checked the head clearance to make sure it would meet the county codes and promptly left. A couple of weeks later the stairway arrived.

I gave quite a bit of thought to designing areas in the house that would accommodate a special set-up for entertainment equipment; record player, compact disk player, stereo speakers, and TV. In the great-room, I planned that the TV would fit into a well in the wall. I also wanted TV jacks in each room so that all TVs would be able to plug into an antenna. A hall closet was designed to accommodate a radio receiver amplifier, record player and record storage. Because I was a little fussy about the audio equipment, I decided to do the installation myself. I bought a quality antenna, installed it in the attic, and ran wires through the walls to each room with a plug-in receptacle. The stereo speakers were designed to hang from the ceiling in the great-room, so I had to reinforce the ceiling area where they would attach with a couple of pieces of wood. This gave a secure mounting for the brackets which would hold the speakers. All of the wiring for this equipment was in place before the inside drywall went up and therefore none of it would have to be installed as an afterthought.

Wells called his heating and air conditioning contractor, and they promised to have a proposed contract to me soon. The basic price would be about $5,400 but there would be extra charges if I wanted the high efficiency heater, electronic air filter and humidifier. I told him I wanted all of them but needed a better handle on the price before making any decisions. After talking to the contractor myself, I was able to get all of the features I wanted for a cost of $6,420. Both Wells' original estimate and the second independent estimate were an identical $8,000, so I came out quite well pricewise.

Some of the windows were not assembled and it fell to the carpenters to assemble and install them. Assembly was time consuming and not at all the high energy action they enjoy. They complained, but by the end of the month all of the first floor windows had been assembled and installed.

July 1   •   NA (No Activity)

July 2   •   Bathtub for the master bath was delivered. The plumbers, who happened to be working that day, slid it from the truck to the bathroom.

       •   We were approaching the time for "backfill" against the foundation walls. A lot of scrap wood — good future food for termites should it get covered with the backfill — had fallen along the foundation walls. I spent most of the day cleaning out the scrap wood.

July 3   •   Met with the "stair-man" at the house and went over stair requirements. He would furnish custom stairs to fit the stairwell.

       •   Wells said he had contacted his recommended heating and air conditioning contractor and that I would receive a proposal from them soon.

       •   A county inspector arrived and approved the site for backfilling.

July 4   •   Independence Day. NA

July 5   •   Told Wells I was going to the beach for a family reunion and would be back in about a week.

July 6   •   Bulldozer was delivered to the site but no backfilling as yet.

July 7   •   Sunday. Drove to beach.

July 8   •   At beach I called Bill and asked if he had evaluated his bid but he had not.

July 9   •   At beach

July 10   •   At beach I called Bill again — still no evaluation. I also called Wells who said that backfilling had been completed and looked great.

July 11   •   At beach

July 12   •   At beach

July 13   •   Returned from beach. I called Bill and he agreed to reduce his bid on the masonry work from $25,723 to $24,000 which I accepted.

       •   Went to the house and found the backfill had been completed and the windows on the first floor had been installed.

July 14   •   Sunday. Madeline and I went through the house and planned where we wanted to place the electrical outlets, switches, fixtures, etc.

July 15   •   NA

July 16   •   Met with Demper and marked house for electrical installations.

July 17 • NA

July 18 • Met again with Demper and settled some minor problems which had been left hanging at the previous meeting.

• Wells presented me with proposals from the electrician, heating and air conditioning people, and the roofer. They all looked good so I approved them.

July 19 • Heating and air conditioning people as well as electricians worked all day.

July 20 • NA

July 21 • Sunday. The county requires outside walls (including basement walls) to be insulated. This was to be done by installing wooden studs along the back basement foundation wall, ground to ceiling. Some of this wall is below grade level and some is above, I decided to paint the inside wall with masonry waterproof paint where it was below grade level and where wood studs would be placed. Such areas have a tendency to sweat and attract moisture. Therefore I insisted that the studs be of pressure treated rot-resistant wood. I later found out that the county now requires this too.

July 22 • Finished painting basement walls. Demper suggested that he install an attic fan. It would have an automatic thermostat control which would turn on at 105°. He would do this for $150 and I told him to go ahead with it and I would send a check in the mail.

July 23 • Bricklayers, electricians, heating and air conditioning people all working.

• Carpenters putting up studs in basement.

July 24 • Installed wiring for TV and radio antenna.

July 25 • Big storm today stopped all work.

July 26 • Still raining. Steel trusses and corregated sheet steel for installation under porch concrete floor were delivered.

July 27 • NA

July 28 • Sunday. Bricklayers working.

July 29 • Bricklayers and electricians working. Brick work around garage now essentially complete. The garage entrance will work but it is not according to plans. We will have to use a wood door jamb in place of the steel door jamb for the three foot entrance door. I decided not to object since it will look and function all right.

July 30 • Bricklayers and electricians working.

July 31 • Bricklayers working on chimney/fireplace.

• Stairs delivered.

The Month of August

"Hey Charlie, when you thinkin' about movin' in?" It was Binney asking. "I'll tell you Binney, it's going to be Thanksgiving turkey dinner in this house. We can do it!" "We *can* do it, Charlie, but you gotta get Wells off his duff and make sure the materials are here when we need them." "I noticed that, Binney, and from now on when you think you're running out of something, I want you to let me know. If I have time, I'll get it here myself." "Okay Charlie, Thanksgiving hmmmmmmmmmmmm."

There was still a lot of concrete work to be done. It was not just one big job but a number of small ones, each requiring some special condition. The garage floor, screened porch, front entranceway, and the great-room hearth all required concrete. On the outside of the house, there were the front and back sidewalks, as well as several slabs for outside doors. The sidewalks and slabs would all be on fill dirt which settles quite a bit, especially during the first year or two. So I deliberately delayed the outside concrete work on these to give the dirt a chance to settle. If done after the ground settles, the concrete could be expected to hold up through the years without cracking. The garage slab was the most serious problem because it was large and had to hold the weight of two cars, and occasionally even loaded trucks. The earthen floor was about seven feet of fill dirt and had been placed there recently during the backfilling of earth around the house. We knew it could be relied upon only to hold the initial pour of concrete while it set up. Over the years, the fill dirt would most assuredly shrink away, leaving the slab unsupported and subject to cracking. My plans called for a number of masonry columns starting at undisturbed ground and rising up to support the concrete floor. These were to be crisscrossed with steel reinforcing bars (re-bars as they are called). In contrast, Bill had built a single large 3 x 3 foot masonry column in the center of the floor. Wells had re-bars placed across this column in a large cross running from edge to edge of the slab. I told Wells that I did not think that there was enough re-bar to support the floor. He told me that the county inspector had already called him with the same comment. The next day I picked up the extra re-bar and installed it myself — and felt better about it. After doing the same for the other areas, we were ready to pour concrete. The next day Wells showed up at our temporary rented house at breakfast time to tell us they were pouring concrete. He needed a check of $763.50 to pay the concrete finishing crew when their job was completed. I gave him the check and later went over to watch them. I get a funny feeling when I see concrete tumbling out of the mixer truck. Once it starts pouring out there is definitely going to be a permanent concrete monument to something. Look around your neighborhood and you will see a lot of these monuments — some not so good. The secret to good concrete monuments is proper preparation, and I hoped I had taken care of that.

Hagen showed up with his crew and started to install flashing and shingles. Bap! Bap! Bap! They stapled the shingles in place using compressed-air staple guns. Flop! Flop! Flop! A truck extended a long moving belt boom and dropped bundles of shingles right on the roof. While the roofers were there, I tried to install caps on the tops of the chimney flues, "anti-bird cages" I call them. When Hagen saw how clumsy I was on the roof, he offered to put the caps on for me. The whole job went fast and the roof was finished in a few days.

Chimney caps reduce the amount of rain water entering each flue and in addition they prevent birds from nesting at the base. I can't imagine how mockingbird fledglings make the passage up a twenty foot flue before their first flight, but I know that they do it. Hagen offered to install the caps for me and I gratefully accepted.

Wells had found some free fill dirt. Someone was digging a public sewer line a few miles away and they had to get rid of all that extra dirt. Huge trucks started to arrive and the drivers wanted to know where to dump it. I had earlier marked the area for dumping so we got the dirt pretty much where we wanted it. I was relieved to find all this free soil because otherwise it could have been a big expense. I figured the truck drivers must have been paid by the load because they raced in and out without much regard to the surroundings. One truck had its bucket still up as it raced away and managed to snag and break my neighbor's telephone line. Fortunately the phone company responded quickly and I went over to say hello to my neighbor and explain. However, as the day wore on, the loads of dirt turned into loads of boulders, stone, and clay muck. So before we had all the fill we needed, we had to stop them from dumping any more. The plan was to get more fill dirt later on and use it to cover the stones — a plan which eventually worked out all right.

The well-driller came with his huge powerful drilling rig. He placed it over the spot indicated by the county inspector and started to drill. It did not take long; the next day he had capped the well and was gone. I wondered what kind of a water supply we had. The driller told me there was ample water, certainly over ten gallons a minute, and perhaps much more. The well was 220 feet deep but the water at the bottom was muddy.

One morning when I got to the house, the well-pump man was already hard at work making a trench for the water service line which runs from the well to the house. The trench intersection with the basement wall was located as shown on the plans but not where Greenie wanted it. Work was so far along I decided not to ask for a change. He ran the line to the house and punched a hole through the basement wall near where he would install the water storage tank and electrical controls. Electric wires were then run from the controls through the trench to the well. These wires were attached to the submersible electric pump and lowered into the well to a depth of 145 feet, which was twenty feet below the water surface. He said this would probably avoid the muddiest water at the bottom of the well. Using his portable electric generator he turned the pump on and checked out all the components of the system. The water was muddy. The system still had to be hooked up permanently to the house current by the electrician and to the water pipes by the plumber.

We wanted to have a central vacuum system installed so I met with the central vac contractor. He looked the house over and then wrote on a brochure "$835 includes power brush." That was the contract. A few days later they installed the plastic tube system throughout the house. The power vacuum unit was brought in later when the house was more complete.

Wells called to say he was going West to a family reunion and wedding. He would be gone two weeks and asked me to get two county inspections completed so we could proceed with drywalling the inside of the house. The first was a "close-in" inspection largely related to electrical wiring which gets covered when the drywall is installed. The second was a "mechanical" inspection having mostly to do with the heating and air conditioning. This work also gets partly covered when the drywall goes up. I met with Binney and we went over the odds and ends which had to be done before we could pass inspection. The county inspector went through the house and approved it for "close-in." County inspectors show their approval by signing the proper decal and sticking it onto an appropriate spot such as a window. By now the laundry room window was about covered with decals. The heating and air conditioning people arranged for the "mechanical" inspection and upon this approval we were ready for drywalling.

The drywall man, Bottle, turned out to be a pleasant little, round Dutchman. This was a big contrast to his workers who were all in great physical shape and strong as bulls. They worked at an incredible pace and with super accuracy; their work was near perfect. In the garage where the ceilings and walls were high, they walked around on stilts to do their work as easily as on their own feet. Bottle already had all the materials on the job before the inspections were completed. The day after the inspectors gave their approval, the drywall was going up.

Before Wells left, he had gotten the septic tank and drain field subcontractor to dig and place the septic tank and drain lines. Sewage from the house drains into the septic tank where it is worked over naturally by bacteria. When these charming little fellows have done their work, only relatively clean water is left; this flows out from the tank into the drain field where it is absorbed into the ground. Tank and drain lines had to be placed carefully so that they would drain properly and still meet county codes for depth below the ground. I asked Wells if he had gone over these specifications with the subcontractor. Wells said, "You told him, I told him, and the county inspector told him; but he will do the job right anyway." Inspection was made, as required, while the trenches were still open and approval was given. Trenches and septic tank were then covered with dirt and the job was finished. Another sticker on the window.

August, day by day

Aug. 1 • Bricklayers working on chimney and fireplace.
• Went over the heatilator-type fireplace with Bill including fans and outside fresh air for burning.

Aug. 2 • Brickwork for chimney and fireplace completed.

Aug. 3 • Started to install TV antenna in attic.

Aug. 4 • Sunday. Brick layers worked on outside front entrance in preparation for concrete .

Aug. 5 • Carpenters installed stairs in stairwell. They fit perfectly.
• Concrete contractor prepared garage floor, garage closet, screened porch, front entrance and fireplace hearth. Preparation included steel reinforcing for concrete.

Aug. 6 • Electricians working.

Aug. 7 • Electricians working.

- County inspector refused to approve garage for concrete — not enough steel reinforcement.

Aug. 8   • Wells sent for more re-bar which I installed myself. I bought even more and installed that too. Inspector then approved.

Aug. 9   • Wells asked for a check to pay concrete finishers. Concrete work completed.

- Electricians working.
- Roofers worked installing shingles and carpenters installed gable roof ventilators.

Aug. 10   • NA (No Activity)

Aug. 11   • Sunday. Finished installing TV antenna in attic.

Aug. 12   • Roofers working.

- Bought caps for chimney flues and roofers installed them.

Aug. 13   • Well-driller was at the site but could not get to drilling point because of mounds of fill dirt. Wells brought in small bulldozer and pushed the dirt away enough for driller to work. Drilling in progress.

Aug. 14   • Drilling and capping of the well completed.

- Dump trucks bringing in fill dirt but we stopped them when their loads became mostly stones. We will have to cover the stones with dirt when final grading takes place.

Aug. 15   • Bricklayers almost completed their work.

Aug. 16   • Heating and air conditioning contractor installing ductwork.

Aug. 17   • Heating and air conditioning contractor working.

Aug. 18   • Sunday. NA

Aug. 19   • Heating and air conditioning contractor working.

Aug. 20   • Met with central vac contractor.

Aug. 21   • Septic tank/drain field contractor arrived with backhoe. He dug the area for the septic tank and the trenches for the drain lines. After approval by county inspector, installed the septic tank and drain lines.

Aug. 22   • Insulation contractor installing bat insulation in outside walls.

Aug. 23   • Insulation contractor working.

Aug. 24   • Insulation contractor working.

Aug. 25   • Sunday. Met with Wells. He will be gone to a family reunion for two weeks and wants me to get two inspections — close-in and mechanical — which are necessary before drywalling can start.

- Madeline and I went through house and established locations and requirements for electrical outlets, switches, lighting fixtures, etc.

Aug. 26 • Insulation people doing detailed caulking.

Aug. 27 • Well pump contractor had already dug water line trench and started installation when I arrived. The line will enter house at location not desired by plumber. He was so far along that I okayed the location as is.

• Heating and air conditioning contractor working.

• Drywall materials delivered.

• Madeline and I spent the afternoon looking at lighting fixtures and carpeting.

Aug. 28 • Met with Binney and went over carpentry which must be finished before drywall can be completely installed.

• Inspectors approved the septic tank, drain field, and well-pump installation.

Aug. 29 • Met with inspector and he gave his approval for close-in. I confirmed arrangements for the mechanical inspection with the heating and air conditioning contractor.

Aug. 30 • Inspector gave approval for mechanical inspection and said we could now proceed with drywalling.

• Bulldozer operator covered septic tank and drain field.

Aug. 31 • Workers putting up drywall. They work fast!

• Tried unsuccessfully to get in touch with Binney to tell him the carpentry necessary for putting up the drywall was not yet completed.

The Month of September

"Aren't those approved stickers on the window beautiful? I just love to see the whole window covered." It was Wells speaking; he had gotten back from his vacation and we were going over the status of the house. The drywall installation was now well along and it was time to consider the doors and trim. Wells had a man from the lumberyard come to the house and go over the selections with me. I already knew I wanted flush birch doors, but there were other selections to be made, including the front and back exterior doors. These days most doors come prehung, that is, already hinged to the door frame and predrilled for door knobs. We went over each door opening as to size and to which way the door opened (right or left hinged). Then I selected the wooden trim molding for each room, including the baseboard and molding around each door. Normally there would also be trim around the windows, but I chose a different method. At each perimeter I had drywall turn the corner and go straight to the window so no wooden trim was required. These corners incorporate a metal bead that resists denting and chipping. I wanted the windowsills to be of ceramic tile and decided to make a trial installation on one of the closet windows. It not only looked good but I found that I enjoyed working with tile so I decided to install all of them. They turned out handsome, even if I say so.

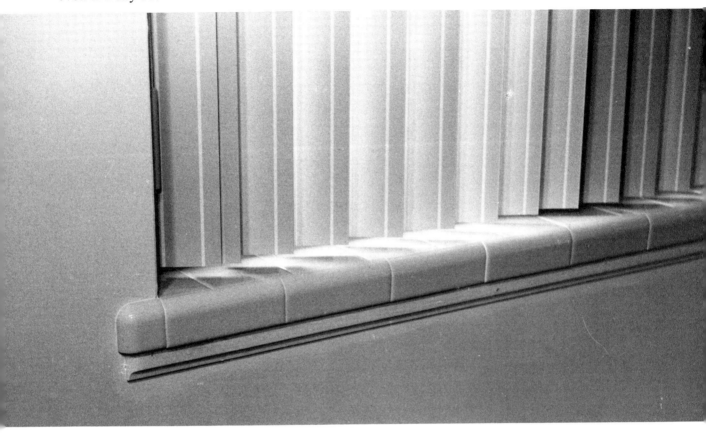

I found that I liked working in tile and that I could do a creditable job of installing the window sills. Madeline liked what she saw so I put tile window sills throughout the house.

The tile wall in back of the stove

The tile sill in the bow window

67

The drywall workers had gotten ahead of the carpenters and had to stop work. I called Binney and he finally got his men out to finish the needed carpentry. One problem was the bow picture window. It was made up of five separate windows bolted together and there were no dimensions in the catalog for the rough wall opening for the assembled window. I called both the local office which had supplied the windows and the home office in Ohio, but neither knew the needed information. I made a small scale drawing of the bow window and then measured the rough opening and gave this to Binney as an approximate dimension. The actual rough opening was to be determined by assembling the window and measuring it. However, at that stage of the construction the work pace was so furious that they did not take time to assemble the window. When it came to nailing up the outside wall frame the carpenter in charge at the time simply took the rough estimate I had given and added a "few inches" to it. As a result the rough opening ended up to be about five inches too small and when the window was assembled it did not fit. The height of the opening was all right but the width was not. The window was installed by centering it to the opening against the *outside* of the house. It looked fine from the outside but I was unhappy with the looks from the inside because the last few inches of the window in the bow were covered by the rough opening which was too small. The situation was remedied by chiseling away some of the wood at the rough opening as shown here:

The chiseling was done; the drywall workers covered it with drywall and it all turned out to be surprisingly good!

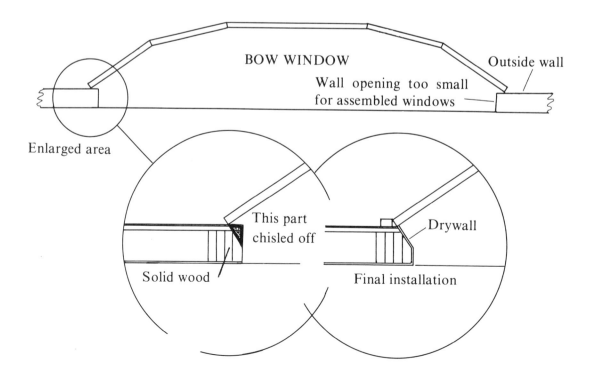

I called Brownie and asked where my bid was on the tile for the bathrooms and entrance hall. He wanted to see for himself what the job entailed so we met at the house and went over the work involved. There were no surprise problems, and his satisfactory bid arrived in the mail a few days later. Tile setters then went to work and soon had most of the bathroom tilework completed.

Madeline was not yet ready to make many of the decisions concerning the interior decorating of the house. She further announced that some choices, such as colors of wall paints, would not be chosen until after we moved in. I decided to go ahead and apply a prime coat of paint to trim, walls and ceilings. When there are no finished floors, carpets or furniture to worry about, it is pleasing to see how fast the prime coat can be rolled on. I would at least have a head start on the painting and Madeline could still pick out her colors and wallpaper later.

In our previous house we had a fine fireplace with a brick wall to the ceiling and a raised brick hearth. One day we had a family gathering and the kids (and some grown-ups too) decided to roast weenies and marshmallows. This was super—just what a good family room fireplace was for. When it was all over (man, was it all over) I noticed that as much hot dog grease had gotten on the brick hearth as had dripped into the fire. A friend commented, "What a great way to antique a new fireplace." I never could get the grease out of the hearth, but I did learn a valuable lesson. I decided to seal and coat the new fireplace brick with a transparent, grease-resistant coating. It now looks very good, and I expect it to stay that way.

Varoom, aroom, aroom! A huge covered truck was backing into the driveway. "Kitchen cabinets," the driver said, "where do you want them?" "The big stuff goes in the living room and the small stuff in the kitchen pantry," I answered. So within an hour we were loaded with little boxes, big boxes, huge boxes and long and short formica counter tops. I was delighted to see the cabinets on site except for one thing. The front and rear doors for the house had not yet been delivered and there was no good way to lock up the house. Kitchen cabinets are especially vulnerable to theft, as are some other things such as appliances and sinks. I called Wells to find out the status of the front and back doors but could not contact him because he was on jury duty. Feeling a little anxious about the situation, I got in touch with Binney about hanging the cabinets. He said that first the kitchen floor needed underlayment (an extra layer of plywood) wherever the vinyl flooring was to go and that he did not have the material at the site to install it. So Binney met me at the lumberyard and loaded the sheets of underlayment on his truck and hauled it to the house. Soon the underlayment went down and installation of the kitchen cabinets got underway.

September, day by day

Sept. 1 • Sunday. Workmen busy installing drywall.

Sept. 2 • Workmen completed all drywall installation they can until carpentry is finished. I called Binney and told him of the problem.

Sept. 3 • Drywall spackling people doing touch-up.
• Madeline and I bought ceiling fan for the great-room.

Sept. 4 • Carpenters working so drywall installers can continue their job.
• Drywall spackling people still working.
• Called Brownie and asked him where the bid for the tilework was. He will meet me and review job at the site tommorow.

Sept. 5 • Met with Brownie and went over the tile job. He had some changes to be made to his bid so I asked him to resubmit it.
• Found an electric wire missing where the light should be over the kitchen sink. The drywall spackling man cut a hole in the drywall and there it was. He fished out the missing wire, positioned it to its correct place, and then patched up the hole he had made.
• Madeline and I started shopping for electrical light fixtures but not much that we liked was available in showrooms.

Sept. 6 • Carpenters finished installing bow picture window. I did not like the looks from the inside and decided to chisel away corner before drywall installation.

Sept. 7 • *Very* hot day! Drywall workmen still spackling and touching up.

Sept. 8 • Sunday. NA (No Activity)

Sept. 9 • Wells returned from his vacation and we went over the status of the house.
• Madeline and I went to electric supply house and selected fixtures mostly from catalog because we saw little that we liked on display.
• Drywall workmen sandpapering walls.

Sept. 10 • Met with Wells and door supplier. I selected interior doors of flush birch and the trim for the inside of the house.
• Went over minor electrical decisions with Demper.

Sept. 11 • Went to electrical fixture supply house and placed an order for fixtures.
• Washed and cleaned brick for fireplace and hearth in preparation for applying grease resistant sealer.

Sept. 12 • Painted brick fireplace and hearth with clear grease resistant sealer.

Sept. 13
- Drywall installed around bow picture window. Looks good.
- Called Wells and reminded him that the steel doors we ordered some time ago had to be picked up. He said he would pick them up soon in his truck.

Sept. 14
- NA

Sept. 15
- Sunday. NA

Sept. 16
- Kitchen cabinet supplier called and said cabinets had arrived from Canada and would be delivered to the house tomorrow. He requested a check which I delivered.
- Wells said that he had gone to pick up steel doors but that they had not been paid for. He forgot to take his check book or he would have paid for them and then collected from me. I gave Wells a check so he could go back and pick them up.
- Madeline and I went to lumberyard and picked out front, back and screened porch doors.

Sept. 17
- Tile setters working in bathrooms.

Sept. 18
- Madeline and I drove to our daughter's house for a visit.

Sept. 19
- Called Wells from daughter's house and told him I would be back in a couple of days.

Sept. 20
- Arrived home from visit. Both upstairs baths almost completely tiled.
- Kitchen cabinets arrived. They were just sitting in a house which could not be locked because there were no outside doors. There is a real danger of theft, although nothing was taken.

Sept. 21
- Went to kitchen cabinet supplier and for my information, discussed cabinet installations. Binney's carpenters are to install them.
- Bought paint supplies from a local Sherwin Williams paint store and started to prime drywall in kitchen.

Sept. 22
- Sunday. Madeline and I painted more drywall.

Sept. 23
- Carpenters finished their job in the garage so drywallers can now complete their work.

Sept. 24
- Workers finished drywall in garage.
- Carpenters started installing some kitchen wall cabinets. Wells had ordered underlayment for kitchen floor but it had not yet been delivered. Binney offered his truck and together we picked it up.

Sept. 25
- Continued to apply prime coat to drywall.

Sept. 26
- Carpenters installed underlayment in kitchen, work room, and kitchen pantry where vinyl floor covering will go.

Sept. 27 • Called Wells and expressed concern over not having outside doors on the house. He checked that morning but they had not yet arrived at the lumberyard.

Sept. 28 • Continued to apply prime coat to drywall.

Sept. 29 • Sunday. Painted prime coat all day.

Sept. 30 • Painted all day. This job went quite fast since there was no finished flooring, furniture, etc., to protect.

The Month of October

Both the interior and exterior doors arrived and were stashed in the great-room where they took up considerable space. In addition, the molding for the interior trim came. Carpenters followed and by the end of the month the doors were hung, and most of the trim was in place. It was not all routine, however, as one day the temporary power suddenly went off and after an hour's waiting the carpenters left for work on another house.

I'm sorry I missed this incident because it must have been spectacular. Our temporary power line ran from the house through a dense hedge and then across an open grass field to the power company's electric transformer. The owner of that grassy field had decided to have it mowed using a big tractor-mower, know in these parts as a "bush hog." Well, you know what happened. The powerful tractor-mower picked up the electric line which was well concealed in the tall grass, and the blades cut it in several places and wound it up into a huge messy ball. I know there were fireworks because of the scorched spots here and there. It all happened before the operator, who surely got a big charge out of it, could shut his machine down. Demper and I reviewed the problem and soon had another line strung so the carpenters could come back to work. I thought I might get a call from the owner but the call never came, perhaps because I had obtained written permission from him earlier to run my temporary power wire across his field.

At this stage of building the carpenters needed to know a remarkable amount of detailed information. They wanted to know the specifics of the trim being placed about the fireplace. They also needed to know the spacing and width of the shelves in the linen closet, pantry, and around the kitchen desk. Wells and I went over all this with Binney and then went to the local lumberyard in Wells' truck and picked up all the needed bits and pieces. I spent the next day or so marking walls as to just where and how I wanted the shelves installed.

The doors were going in and it was time to consider what type of hardware we wanted for them. Madeline and I went to the hardware store recommended by Wells and selected pewter-like door knobs and latches. All the hardware for the exterior doors had matching locks. I thought getting matching locks might be a problem, but I found that it only took a moment for the clerk to set each lock to fit one key. Since I'm fussy about it, I decided to finish the doors myself. Both interior and exterior doors would be sanded and stained followed by three coats of polyurethane varnish.

A large amount of trash had collected both inside and outside the house. Wells had told me of my options on this some time ago. We could have one of those huge metal boxes deposited on the lot. When full, they would load it onto a truck and haul it away. That was the most expensive. Another option was to call a trash removal outfit when the trash pile got big enough. That was less expensive. I called my son Richard who lived a couple of hours drive away, and he agreed to help me with the task. This was least expensive. I made arrangements with a local truck rental for a pickup truck and all was set for clean-up day. Trash dumps could not be found in the yellow pages but I had heard of a place nearby called the "Dump Stump." So in desperation I looked up the name "Dump Stump" and there it was! A lady on the phone said, "It will be ten dollars a load for a pickup truck." When we arrived with the first load we were in for a remarkable sight. The dump was a huge hole in the ground — I mean acres and acres — and we had to drive down long carved dirt ramps along the side of the hole to get to the bottom. It was a bee hive of activity including eighteen wheelers, dump trucks, cars with trailers, pickup trucks like mine, and just plain cars loaded with junk. Dodging some pretty big vehicles, we made our way to the bottom and deposited our trash, making a pile so relatively small as to be unnoticeable. At the bottom there were bulldozers constantly moving trash into more compact positions. Everything imaginable was there, including some brand new items. It is rumored that, on occasion, the Russian Embassy dumps papers here and later people come and remove them for whatever purpose I do not know. We had a pretty good mix of trash ourselves, and after five loads and a hard day's work we finished this unpleasant task.

More truck loads of fill dirt started to arrive. Wells had found some more free dirt and I was glad to see it. This time it was real dirt — not stones as before — and we could use it to cover the stone which had been dumped earlier. Wells arranged for a bulldozer and set out some grade stakes to guide the operator. A few days later the bulldozer was busy leveling the old pile of stones and covering them with dirt. The operator complained that he needed ten more loads but Wells decided that there was enough dirt on hand so the operator had to make do with what we had. Then five loads of gravel arrived and were dumped where the driveway, parking, and turn around areas were to be. Again the bulldozer transformed the formidable looking piles of gravel into a more friendly sight.

The side loading garage necessitated a lot of extra fill dirt. Do you see a thousand cubic yards of fill? It's all there!

No sooner had the bulldozer finished grading than the electric power company arrived, set a new pole and ran the underground power line from the pole to the back of the house where the meter was installed. They tore up the ground pretty well and left some humps, which I promptly leveled with shovel and rake.

Wells called to say that he was unable to get his usual fine-grading and grass-seeding crew to schedule my house in the near future. Would I want to do it with his help? We would rent a tractor-rake to help with the fine grading. So Wells showed up in his truck and we drove to a nearby seed store where we bought grass seed and straw. Wells explained that the county inspector would not issue an occupancy permit unless the soil around the house had been "stabilized." We spent the rest of the day raking and seeding so that by nightfall about three-quarters of the job was complete. The next day Madeline and I finished the job. I raked and spread straw while she walked back and forth with a hand-cranked seed spreader. At first I think she was a little timid over operating the seeder, but when she got on to it and saw how smoothly it gobbled up the seed and how evenly it spread it, she began to think it was fun. The next day it rained and the yard became a sea of mud. It was a little late in the year to be planting grass seed and the yard stayed that way until the seed slowly and reluctantly popped up. Looking at the yard with the tender seedlings starting to show, Wells said, "I think that's good enough for the inspector to pass it." He was right.

Madeline found an over-the-stove combination microwave and exhaust fan unit. It was on sale at a good price so she bought it.

On the last day of the month a big truck arrived and dumped stacks of rough cedar plywood and long strips of solid cedar. The strips would be used for vertical battens and trim, and the plywood would be used for siding. It would be up to the carpenters to cut, fit and fasten this material to the outside of the house to give it its final appearance.

October, day by day

Oct. 1 • The doors arrived and were placed in the living room. They were all prehung and all had three hinges which I liked (interior doors usually only have two hinges and these do not resist warping as well as three hinges.)

• Madeline and I went to the local hardware supply store and picked out the hardware for both inside and outside doors.

Oct. 2 • Painted all day.

Oct. 3 • Painted all day.

Oct. 4 • Carpenters started to install doors. When temporary power went off they left to work on another job.

Oct. 5 • Found that the temporary electric line had been cut by mowing equipment in a field nearby. I then met with Demper and figured out what needed to be done to repair damage.

Oct. 6 • Sunday. New temporary power line installed.

Oct. 7 • Carpenters installing doors.

Oct. 8 • Carpenters completed installing doors and started on trim around door frames.

Oct. 9 • Made a list of the many pieces of trim, shelving, etc. that the carpenters needed. Wells and I took his truck to the lumberyard, picked it up, and delivered it to the house.

Oct. 10 • Carpenters working on trim. They need information on placement of shelves in closets, pantry and desk well.

Oct. 11 • Marked all the walls for the position of shelves, as the carpenters had asked.

Oct. 12 • Sanded and stained the front and back outside doors.
• Wells found some more free dirt and the loaded trucks started to show up. I directed them where to dump.

Oct. 13 • Sunday. Madeline painted trim while I stained interior doors.

Oct. 14 • Rented a pickup truck and son Richard and I hauled the trash (a great amount had accumulated by now) from around the house and hauled it to the dump. Hard work!

Oct. 15 • Wells said it was now time to do final grading of the dirt we had collected so he and I set grade stakes to guide the bulldozer operator.

Oct. 16 • The bulldozer arrived but actual grading was set up for the following day.
• Madeline continued to paint trim and I continued to sand, stain and varnish doors.

Oct. 17 • Bulldozer started the grading but the operator said he needed ten more loads of dirt. Wells did not agree and gave instructions to the operator on how to make do with what we had.

Oct. 18 • Bulldozer still grading. Gravel for driveway arrived and bulldozer spread it as planned. Grading was finished by nightfall and the bulldozer was trailered away.

Oct. 19 • Madeline and I met with carpet supplier and reviewed samples.

Oct. 20 • Sunday. NA (No Activity)

Oct. 21 • Carpenters worked installing shelving. They needed a few more supplies which I got for them.
• A cold rain fell all day and night which made the grounds around the house a mess of mud. Only the gravel drive allows access to the house.

Oct. 22 • Carpenters still installing shelves and trim.
• Went to hardware store and bought closet clothes rods. Carpenters installed them.

Oct. 23 • Madeline and I spent the day reviewing kitchen appliances and purchased a combination hood-microwave unit for over the stove.

Oct. 24 • Carpenters worked installing the five outside metal doors. One of the matching metal jambs of these doors was missing so carpenters made a wooden jamb (frame) for it. A few weeks later I found the metal jamb in the tall grass by the garden but I never found out how it got there.

Oct. 25 • Heating and air conditioning people busy installing equipment.
• Electric power people arrived and installed the permanent power line from a nearby pole to the meter at the back of the house. While placing the line in the trench they tore up some of the grading the bulldozer had done a few days earlier. I regraded the rough areas by hand.

Oct. 26 • Painted most of the day.

Oct. 27 • Sunday. Again painted most of the day.

Oct. 28 • Heating and air conditioning people worked installing furnace.
• Wells could not schedule his usual fine grading and seeding crew. If I wanted, Wells and I could do it together with the help of a rented tractor-rake. I agreed that he and I should do it.

Oct. 29 • Wells and I went in his truck and purchased grass seed and straw.
• We met the tractor-rake man at the house, and went to work. By nightfall all the raking was done and over half the seeding and straw cover was completed. Rain scheduled for tomorrow.

Oct. 30 • Raked and spread straw while Madeline spread seed with a hand cranked seed-spreader which worked quite well. The forecasted rain did not materialize and we almost finished the job.
• The gas people arrived and marked the path for the gas line from the main road to the meter location on the back of the house.
• Madeline and I drove to local floor covering store and made final selection of vinyl floor for kitchen, pantry and workroom.
• Bathroom cabinets, which I had ordered unfinished, arrived at the house and were placed in the master bedroom.

Oct. 31 • Stacks of rough cedar plywood for siding along with the solid wood cedar trim arrived.

The Month of November

It was getting colder now, and the grounds about the house were awfully muddy but the little grass seedlings kept popping through. By month's end we had a green "peach fuzz" yard — enough to hold the ground and prevent appreciable erosion over the winter.

I met with Wells and told him that his estimate of moving into the house in thirty-two weeks did not look realistic to me and he agreed. The end of Wells' thirty-second week was only about two weeks away. Although he had suffered some unfortunate personal delays, such as his accident in April, I did not feel that I should have to pay his $500 a week fee beyond his thirty-two week estimate. In my opinion that was enough time to complete the house. I stated my feelings to Wells and proposed that I end my payments to him at the end of his time estimate. He agreed and said that he did not expect any additional payment beyond the thirty-two weeks. He also promised to continue his services until we moved in and even after that if I should need him. I felt relieved by Wells' position, although I believe that I could have completed the house on my own if it had come to that; fortunately it did not.

Between the hall and the open stairwell, a bannister was to be prominently in view. However, Madeline did not like any of the sketches I showed to her. "Well," she said, "I know I don't like any of those spindly fancy dust-catching picket fences you are showing me." We ended up at the lumberyard going through their catalogs, but nothing would do. Finally I said, "Wells is putting up a modern house with a lot of bannister work in it, maybe you would like his design." His bannisters were a much refined version of the handrail-picket designs you see on some outdoor decks, only they were made of clear oak wood, with pegged screw attachments, and were carefully sanded and varnished. Wow! That was it! So back we went to the lumberyard and ordered enough rectangular pickets (balusters), a heavy handrail, and a special piece for a newel post — all in clear oak. When the materials arrived at the house, I could not help but admire the beautiful wood. I was pleased until I saw the bill for almost $500 — and it had not yet been installed! It's less than ten feet long and I figure it to be one of the more expensive trappings in the house. It is beautiful, although I'm just now starting to enjoy it.

There are other railings too. The county requires railings along most steps where there are three or more risers. The brick steps at the front door have three risers and had to have railings which I elected to have installed in wrought iron. I liked this job because it was done so quickly and with good results.

The contract for the custom iron railings at the front door was handled verbally. I explained what I wanted to the supplier and a couple of weeks later the railings were in place (along with the bill).

One day the gas company showed up with their equipment and dug a trench for the gas pipe from the road to the house. "Where is the meter?" I asked. "No meter until the inside piping is installed, inspected, and approved," the gas boss said. When the plumber saw where the gas pipe was to enter the house he was mad. According to his judgment it should have entered the house at the opposite end, nearer the furnace. He moaned that he would have to charge for an extra hundred feet of gas pipe because it had not been included in his bid, and the same for the water pipe which did not enter the house where he had asked for it. I did not like opening up his contract to more unknown costs but it was the only reasonable course. He said he would keep track of his extra labor and materials and add it on to the cost of his contract. I said I hoped he would. I think he did just that because the extra charge was not great. Cold weather was setting in, and his work was essential to getting the heat turned on in the house.

A big boxy truck rolled into the driveway, popping some branches off the trees lining the roadway. It was the crew to blow the insulation into the attic. Fellows with masks swarmed into the house and with a huff and puff they were done and gone.

Carpenters were busy installing the rough cedar plywood siding and vertical battens. It went up rather quickly and the outside of the house began to take on a finished appearance.

A previous house I built also used some rough cedar siding and vertical battens. On that house I had elected to use solid cedar boards instead of plywood. The battens, of course, covered the vertical cracks between the boards. If nailed in place with bright (uncoated) nails the chemical action between wood, metal nails, and moisture soon produces a dark stain at each nail head called "weeping." A usual way of avoiding this problem is to "set" each nail head, that is, drive the nail head below the wood surface and then cover the depression with putty before painting. This takes time but it does avoid the weeping problem. However, if the wood is left to weather or is slightly stained, the putty may produce an undesirable visible spot at each nail head. Previously, I had weather-tested some cedar siding using aluminum nails and found no weeping. Unfortunately, in order to have the strength of their steel counterpart, aluminum nails are made greater in diameter. Many splits in the solid wood resulted, especially in the battens. Some of the splits took months to appear. Although generally satisfactory, the aluminum nails did not produce a condition as good as I had hoped for. Stainless steel nails may be an expensive alternate but I have not tested them. Where wood siding was to be used on the present house, I decided to require rough cedar plywood because it greatly resists splitting. Solid wood vertical battens would be fastened in place with steel galvanized nails that had not been "set." Wells advised that this was probably the best combination although I still have reservations about the galvanized nails. If they start to weep in a few years I may have to set each nail, then putty and paint.

Uncoated (bright) nail heads
weeping in redwood.

The carpenters had the siding and battens mostly installed by the end of the month. They put up the scaffolding and did their job in spite of the ever resisting mud around the house. Also during this period they finished most of the interior trim.

Madeline and I had selected and ordered the hardware for the doors but when time for delivery came we found that our selection was out of production and not available. We made a second selection and this time it was delivered and promptly installed by the carpenters.

Floor coverings such as the sheet vinyl we had chosen required a special underlayment over the subflooring. This second layer of plywood was laid down over the rough subflooring and screwed into place *every six* inches. The screws were driven so that the heads were sunk just below the plywood surface. Small depressions left by the screws show through the vinyl if not filled with dabs of "flash patch." Cracks also needed to be filled so they would not show through. I did the flash patch work myself and then sandpapered it so that it would be a good job. Underlayments for the vinyl floor were installed in the kitchen, pantry, and workroom. The floor was similarly prepared with an underlayment where ceramic tile was to be installed in the entrance hall and bathrooms, except here the flash patch was not necessary.

Having about completed the cedar siding on the house, it was time to put up the frames to support the screening on the screened porch. I did not want these exposed frames to rot in the future so I decided to make them of redwood which naturally resists rotting. I measured the job and explained it to the carpenter, who understood it very well. Then I bought the thick (5/4 inch) strips, some short, some long, as needed for the job, and unloaded them onto the porch floor. When I got back from lunch, the carpenters had changed crews and the new lead man, not having been briefed, was just cutting the last of the long strips into short pieces. He said, "I need more long lengths to do this job." I was about ready to explode, but I held my temper and went back to the lumberyard and bought the long strips all over again.

Screened porch

While painting, Wells put me on to a good procedure for baseboard trim. This is the wood molding that faces between interior walls and floor. Although nailed securely to the walls it still moves a little from summer to winter and invariably develops an unsightly crack between the wall and the top of the molding. A bead of caulking forced into this crack or joint effectively seals it permanently. The new caulkings, developed for outside use, retain their flexibility throughout their life. Caulkings are applied with a caulking gun and the work goes quickly. I caulked the baseboard throughout the house.

November, day by day

Nov. 1   •   Gave doors first coat of varnish. I had previously sandpapered and stained them. Because the interior doors are flush, that is, they have no panels or carving, I was able to apply the varnish (polyurethane) with a roller as this is much faster than brushing it on. The exterior doors were paneled so I had to brush the varnish on these and it took a lot of time. The final finish would consist of three coats of varnish with sanding between coats.

Nov. 2   •   Continued to varnish doors. The bathroom cabinets arrived and I had purchased them unfinished because Madeline had not made up her mind as to the bathroom decor. Besides, they came less expensive when unfinished. I sanded them and gave them their first coat of white enamel, the color Madeline had decided on. It would take three coats of white enamel to complete this job. I also finished the interiors of these cabinets with clear varnish.

Nov. 3   •   Sunday. Painted second coat of enamel on bathroom cabinets and also painted bathroom walls and ceilings in preparation for wallpapering.

Nov. 4   •   Rain, Rain! I helped apply the flash-patch to cover the screw heads in kitchen, workroom, and pantry floors in preparation for the sheet vinyl flooring.

Nov. 5   •   Rain, Mud! Completed preparation for vinyl floor covering.

Nov. 6   •   Rain ending. Sanded doors to prepare for second coat of varnish.

          •   The crew to install the gas line showed with trucks and trenchers but left because grounds were too muddy.

Nov. 7   •   NA (No Activity)

Nov. 8   •   Carpenters started to apply rough cedar plywood siding. Gas line crew arrived and installed the gas line, leaving a fairly rough cut and re-fill through the graded and seeded yard.

Nov. 9 • Fine-graded and seeded the roughly covered trench left from the gas line installation.

Nov. 10 • Sunday. Continued to sand and varnish doors.

Nov. 11 • Carpenters continued to install siding. They needed four triangular ventilators to install in the peaks of each gable. Wells said he would get them there the next morning but I offered to pick them up immediately, which I did.

• Discussed briefly with Wells the end of our agreement but drew no conclusions. Since I was renting a house to live in while we were building it was time to give the landlord notice of our departure. Our discussion gave me a notion of when I might expect to move in — it looked like about January 1.

• There had been a mistake in the estimated amount of siding and batten strips delivered so a new estimate of the materials still needed was made and the order was placed with the lumberyard. Carpenters could not work further until these materials were delivered.

Nov. 12 • Continued to varnish doors.

Nov. 13 • Continued varnishing doors. Still no delivery from the lumberyard, even though it was promised yesterday.

Nov. 14 • Wells and I went in his truck to a nearby stone quarry and picked up stepping stones. These go from the gravel parking area to the front door. They were heavy and weighed his truck down so that we drove home slowly. Wells and I laid them in place.

• Madeline and I drove to another house Wells was building to see a modern bannister he had installed. She had not liked any other designs I had shown her but she did like this one. We then drove to the lumberyard and ordered the materials. While there I asked about the siding materials we needed so much and they promised to deliver them tomorrow.

• Drove to the hardware supplier and placed the order for the interior and exterior door hardware.

Nov. 15 • Gave the doors their third and last coat of varnish — they look good!

• Lumberyard finally delivered the siding materials. They drove in with a huge truck, tilted up the back and slid the big plywood sheets right off into the mud. Wells just said, "That's the way they do it."

● The hardware supplier called and said that the hardware we had ordered was out of production and out of stock so we would have to make another selection.

Nov. 16 ● A man from the ornamental iron shop met with me and went over the job for iron railings at the front door. He was only there a few minutes, made some measurements, and quoted me a price which I accepted. He would do the job and send me the bill.

Nov. 17 ● Sunday. NA

Nov. 18 ● Carpenters continued to install siding. They also installed the finished cabinets in the bathrooms.

● Madeline and I went to the hardware supplier but were unable to make an alternate selection for door hardware.

Nov. 19 ● The insulation people blew insulation into the attic. It did not take long.

● Carpenters busy installing siding. I called the power company and said we were about ready for permanent power hookup. They had nothing scheduled for us but would look into it.

● Grass seedlings are up!

Nov. 20 ● Many carpenters worked installing siding.

● Drove to the lumberyard and picked up the redwood strips for the screened porch frames and gave them to the carpenters. In their headlong way they cut up the long strips first and I had to go back and buy more long strips to complete the job.

● Madeline went to the hardware supplier and decided on the door hardware and ordered it.

Nov. 21 ● Picked up hardware and gave it to carpenters for installation.

● Called the power company but they will not promise installation of permanent power to the house before November 27th.

● Carpenters have about completed the outside siding and trim and have started putting screening on the porch.

● Continued to paint prime coat on interior trim.

Nov. 22 ● Greenie called and grumbled over the fact that the gas pipe and also the water pipe from the well enter the house at different locations than he wanted. I explained the way that came about but that did not make him happy. "I'll take account of the extra time and materials," he said, "and add it on to the cost."

● Binney said, "This door hardware for the back door does not fit. You got a long keeper and the door was drilled for a short one." So I went back to the hardware supplier to exchange the long keeper for the short. I could have handled all of these things through Wells but it would entail more time which I wanted to avoid, seeing that winter had started to show and I had given notice to the landlord where we rented that we would end our lease on Jan. 4th.

- Called both the tile contractor and the carpet contractor and tried to arrange an early but compatible installation date (the front entrance foyer tile interfaces with the carpeting).

Nov. 23
- Continued to paint trim prime coat.

Nov. 24
- Sunday. Since Madeline had still not committed on the kitchen decor, I decided to paint the kitchen with a final two coats of semi-gloss white. This will render the kitchen fully usuable and still allow wallpapering, which she probably will want after we move in. I painted semi-gloss white in the kitchen and pantry.

Nov. 25
- The power company truck arrived and placed a new pole for the power line. It is placed adjacent to an old pole which will be removed when the lines are transferred to the new pole.
- Mirrors for the bathrooms arrived. They would be very vulnerable until they were in place on the bathroom walls.

Nov. 26
- Plumbers worked today installing the gas line and water lines inside the house. Greenie grumbled that they did not enter the house where he wanted but he kept track of the extra time and material as promised. He also wanted to move the hot water heater to the opposite side of the chimney column because it fit better there. A flue ran by the new location (it's a gas heater and requires a flue) but there was no opening through the brick. Greenie would not cut the hole through the brick and Bill would take a couple of days to get to it. So I got out my trusty mason's chisel and cut it out myself and saved the time. It is a much better installation than the one originally planned.
- Wells said that we now must go for three major inspections before we can apply for an occupancy permit from the county: plumbing inspection, which Greenie will apply for; mechanical, which the heating and air conditioning people apply for; and electrical, which Demper will apply for.

Nov. 27
- Greenie called and said that the inspector had approved the plumbing. I then called the gas people and they said that they would install the meter December 2.

Nov. 28
- Thanksgiving Day. We were supposed to be in the house by now. Instead I painted and also found enough vinyl left over from the floor to line the shelves in the pantry. It had been raining and it was cold and damp working in the house. More grass was showing.

Nov. 29   • The lumberyard delivered the materials for the bannister. It was beautiful clear oak, but the price was much more than I had expected. Binney came with a crew and removed the scaffolding from around the outside of the house since the siding application had been completed.

Nov. 30   • Did more painting inside. House was *cold*.
• Demper turned on the house current although everything electric had not yet been hooked up.

The Month of December

It wasn't getting colder anymore, it was just plain cold. We were occasionally getting some snow and slippery roads, all of which were discouraging to doing detailed work inside. Then on December 5th the heat was turned on. Aaaah! What a relief! Work that had turned into a frigid struggle melted back into pleasurable effort. The warmth didn't just increase the temperature in the house, it penetrated into our bones because we knew now that "moving in" time was nearly here.

Locks on the outside doors were finally installed. There was now a considerable amount of expensive equipment sitting around the house and it was a relief to know that we could at least lock the doors. We had not lost anything to thieves but others nearby certainly had. Maybe we were just lucky or maybe I had been at the house enough to discourage thieves; in any case the doors being locked made me feel better. It also meant that I had to get up each morning to unlock the doors before seven which is usually the hour for contractors to start work.

Tile setters had refused to work anymore until the heat was turned on so I called and gave them the "go ahead." The morning they were to start work I arrived at the house early and unlocked the doors, then went home to the rented house for breakfast. When I got back to the building site, the first two courses of tile had been laid in the entrance foyer but they were the wrong color! That particular tile comes in three shades of tan: light, medium and dark. Madeline had ordered light and they were installing medium. My eyes are somewhat color insensitive and I don't trust my view in these matters, so I asked them to hold while I got a reading from the "color boss." Madeline was just finishing her breakfast and when I described what happened, she was dismayed, mad, and a few other things. I said, "I knew you wouldn't like it but I just need a decision. We can tear out what they have done and make them put in what you ordered which will entail some delay, or we can let them proceed. I think it looks okay." She had not expected to be confronted with decisions at this early hour, but her final decision was to proceed. Now when I sit in the great-room and look at the tile foyer, I think it looks even better than the lighter tile.

A bannister can be a thing of beauty and I aimed to have one. But I also wanted it to be safe. It seems to me that in many modern homes the newel posts come loose and weaken from working back and forth during normal use. Besides a feeling of insecurity, I wonder what the national statistics would show about such conditions causing serious accidents. I wanted a secure and strong bannister in my house, one that would not come loose. I insisted that the newel post and all balusters be secured to the basic house structure just below floor level. This way the rail would be like a rock. Taken aback a little at first, the carpenters were eventually pleased with my decision and work went on to complete the job as I wished.

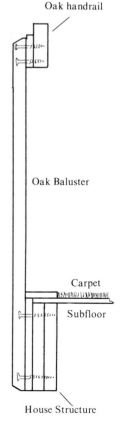

I insisted that the banister be securely mounted so that it would not wobble or become loose through use.

87

The firm, but expensive bannister

One day the vinyl floor people showed up and in very little time installed the floor in the kitchen, pantry and work room. There was a lot of vinyl leftover and I measured the extra and found that I could line the surface of the shelves in the kitchen pantry and those above the kitchen desk as well. So I surfaced these shelves with the leftover vinyl using a permanent adhesive and then faced each shelf edge with an oak strip to match the oak trim on the kitchen cabinets. The surface of each shelf was then permanent, clean, and scrubbable.

Greenie came with his crew of two sons and hooked up the kitchen sink, bathroom sinks, bathtubs and shower. He said that the tile platform for the master bathroom tub was too high and that he had to drive the attachment fittings up through the tiles, so that threads for the water spout would catch. In doing so, he had broken some tiles and I had to call Brownie back to replace them. Apparently, this is not unusual because Brownie neither complained nor asked for extra money for the job.

I had selected a double laundry tub for the laundry room because I know that Madeline likes to drip-dry some things by hanging them over the tub. The overhead clothes rod can be only the width of the tub, otherwise the drippings may go elsewhere. Accordingly, in the house plans, I had laid out the room width to accept the washer, dryer and double tub, plus three inches for inaccuracies. As it happened, the detailed dimensions added up against me. The actual room dimension was a fraction of an inch too short, and after a talk with Greenie, he agreed to take back the double tub and furnish a single tub. A little frustrated, Greenie asked, "Now that I've got it, who the hell am I gonna sell this double tub to?" I figured I had no business answering. So it happened that I planned a double tub but got a single tub.

The microwave oven combined with an over-the-stove hood unit was delivered about the same time as the stove and dishwasher. Then the refrigerator was delivered but I was alone and the two men who delivered it would not, perhaps could not, carry it into the kitchen. It sat in the garage for a few days until some neighbors wandered over to see how the house was progressing. There were four men including myself and we easily lifted it and set it in its place in the kitchen. Would I call Greenie to hook up the water tube for the ice maker? No, he was getting upset enough with me, so I hooked it up myself.

When I arrived to open the house one morning, the crew to install the gutters and downspouts were already at work. I had gone over the job with their lead man several days before. These were extruded aluminum seamless continuous gutters formed from big rolls of flat strip aluminum right on the job site. Aside from their function of carrying off the rain water from the roof, the gutters form a very visual roof line for the whole house. They used to be made of short lengths of galvanized iron guttering soldered together to get the needed longer lengths. The short pieces were almost always misaligned and I found the resulting slightly cockeyed roof line on previous houses to be annoying. It is much harder to misalign the continuous gutters, but it can still happen. Look around your neighborhood and you will see. Then the foreman said, "You wanted a gutter on the apron roof on the back of the house, I hope." I said, "No, I had not planned on one there," but went back to see it and decided it looked pretty good. He had previously quoted me a price per lineal foot of gutter plus splash plates. Guttering is suprisingly inexpensive and I knew that a small cost increment was involved so I said okay and let it go at that.

I had not planned to have a gutter on the apron roof. By the time I got to the house that morning the gutter contractor had already installed it. It looked good so I let it stay.

Carpeting people were scheduled to install the carpet in just two days. It occurred to me that the subflooring was dirty and full of bumps because of the globs of joint compound dropped by the drywall installers. I called the carpet boss and he said that they normally do not clean the floor or remove minor bumps because with the under-carpet padding, nothing shows. It took me an extra day of scraping and vacuuming bumps before I was satisfied. When they got to installing, the work went quite fast but ended with the job partly finished for lack of carpet. The boss arrived and told them there had been enough carpet for the job. Mentally I flashed back to the wood for the screened porch, but I said nothing. My contract was a fixed-price, so after some delay they came back with the extra carpet and finished the job. There were more than a few short carpet strips left over.

It was time to install electrical fixtures, but the supplier could only make a partial delivery because he could not get everything he had ordered from the manufacturers, even though we had confirmed our order and made a deposit several months ago. A partial delivery was made. The supplier usually does not install — that's the electrician's job. Demper and his crew did the installation, but said that the electrical inspection was due and the house would not pass unless all fixtures were put in. I called the fixture supplier and told him of the dilemma. He tried to resolve this by supplying temporary fixtures; final fixtures would replace temporary ones later and the supplier would put them up instead of Demper. When Demper finished installing the temporary fixtures, there were still five missing. I finally went to the local hardware store and bought five "keyless" fixtures (bare-light porcelain fixtures) and Demper installed them.

Demper said that in his opinion, there were two fixtures which the electrical inspector might not approve. One was a closet light which could not be installed in the normal ceiling position because a sheet metal heat duct had been run across that area and consequently the ceiling had been dropped a foot or so. As a result, the light fixture had been placed in the wall but it was still less than eighteen inches from the closet shelf which violated the county code (potential fire hazard). I found the shortest bulb available and screwed it in. It measured about sixteen inches from the shelf and I decided to let it go at that. The second was a light fixture located on the wall in back of the tub in the master bath. By stretching, one could reach the fixture while standing in the tub which is a "no-no." We placed a blank cap over the electrical opening, and I hung a large mirror over it. A few days later Demper called for the county electrical inspection, and another approval sticker went up.

Demper turned on the pump for the first time. It worked and we had water — hot water too! The sinks worked, as did the toilets. I called the portable john people and told them to discontinue their service. Greenie informed me that the county inspector had approved the plumbing. The heating contractor called and said that the county mechanical inspection had been made and was approved. Binney came with his crew and finished the inside and outside trim work, closet shelves, clothes rods, etc. Finally, Wells said I should apply for the occupancy permit! However, it was late in the month now and I told Wells that we may not get the occupancy permit before we move in. He said the county can impose a fine of $1,000 a day for each day that the occupancy permit is violated, but they almost never enforce it. It didn't make me feel any better.

By the end of the month we had started to move personal things from the rented house to the new house: stereo equipment, TVs, musical instruments, chinaware, shop machines, anything we did not want movers to touch. It was a relief not to have to move everything in one day as we had to do when we moved into the rented house.

I called the county and applied for an occupancy permit. A few days later I met the inpsector at the front door. Seeing the things we had moved in he said, "Oh ho! You've moved in on me already!" I said, "No, we have moved some things but we still occupy a rental house nearby." We went through the house in detail and all was in order until we came to the garage and screened porch area. He said, "Here we have a garage attached to the house and the fire code says that the house must be separated from the garage by fire-rated materials such as fire-rated doors and drywall. Bottle had used fire-rated drywall where he had thought it was necessary. "Your entrance to the garage from the kitchen is through the screened porch door and we will not allow this. You must place fire-rated drywall around the screen door frame and replace the screen door with a fire-rated door." I told him he was "uglifying" my design but that I would make the change and call him back as soon as the job was done.

This all took place about Christmastime and we had, of course, expected to be living in the house by now. Not to be denied a Christmas celebration with family, we invited them anyway to a housewarming holiday dinner in the new house the day after Christmas. The only ones missing would be daughter Ann and her family who live in the state of Washington. The day came and it was a great family housewarming indeed with children and grandchildren. Madeline prepared an elegant dinner, and we enjoyed it in the glow of the fireplace in the great-room, incomplete as it was. When the night grew late we split up, some sleeping in the rented house and some in sleeping bags on the carpet in front of the fireplace. The dream house was awakening.

December, day by day

Dec. 1 • Sunday. NA (No Activity)

Dec. 2 • Carpenters working on trim and details. They installed locks on outside doors.

- Gas company set the gas meter.

Dec. 3
- Partial delivery of electric light fixtures made today.
- Worked on bannister.

Dec. 4
- Freezing weather. Heating contractor installed flues from furnace to chimney.

Dec. 5
- Heating contractor turned on heat for the first time — and it felt great!
- Carpenters putting up screened porch frames.

Dec. 6
- Carpenters putting up bannister and completed screen porch.
- Electricians turned on water pump.
- Plumbers completed hooking up sinks and bathtubs. They broke several tiles around tub in master bathroom.
- Tried to install double washtub but it would not fit in the available space. I agreed to exchange it for a single tub.
- Changed location of hot water heater to opposite side of chimney but this would entail knocking hole through chimney wall to connect with the flue on that side of the chimney. Plumber refused to knock hole in chimney. Rather than wait for mason to schedule the work, I did it myself.
- Finished final coat of paint for all ceilings in house.

Dec. 7
- Carpenters working on trim details inside and outside.
- Screw plugs being installed in bannister.

Dec. 8
- Sunday. Dishwasher uncrated and set in place — now ready for electrical and plumbing hookup.

Dec. 9
- Finished installing thimble in chimney hole in flue.
- Carpenters finished installing bannister.

Dec. 10
- Tile setters started to install wrong color tile in entrance foyer. I stopped them until Madeline gave her okay.

Dec. 11
- Plumber hooked up kitchen sink, hot water heater, and dishwasher.
- Called county and requested water test. They will only draw water from the kitchen sink so we had to wait until today before we could request a test.
- Sanded and stained bannister.

Dec. 12
- Electric fixture supplier furnished substitute fixtures since he could not get the ones we ordered.
- Electricians installing fixtures. Fixture supplier to furnish and install final fixtures when he gets them. Madeline called moving people and made date to move us from rented house on Jan. 2.
- Varnished the bannister.

Dec. 13 • Still five electric fixtures short so I bought five keyless (bare light porcelain) fixtures which the electrician installed.

Dec. 14 • Electrician said that two fixtures might not pass electrical inspections, a closet bulb (too close to the shelf) and a fixture near the master bathroom bathtub. I bought a very short bulb for the closet and hung a mirror over the one in the bathroom.

• Carpet supplier advised that they do not clean floors before installing carpet.

Dec. 15 • Sunday. Madeline and I cleaned floors in preparation for carpet installation.

Dec. 16 • Inspector came and took water sample for testing from kitchen sink.

• Carpet installers started but ran short. They will need more carpet and there will be a delay.

Dec. 17 • Hung doors on bathroom cabinets.

• Installed vinyl on pantry shelves.

Dec. 18 • Electrical inspection was made and approved.

• Plumbing inspection awaiting results of water tests.

• Continued to install vinyl on pantry shelves.

Dec. 19 • Finished vinyl installation on pantry shelves and also installed oak facing on edge of shelves.

Dec. 20 • Snow today and slick roads.

• Refrigerator delivered today.

Dec. 21 • Madeline cleaned bathrooms and I installed trim around kitchen stove.

Dec. 22 • Sunday. We started to move some things from the rented house to the new house. Moved dining room set since we plan to have a family dinner there on December 26.

• Hung the stereo speakers on the great-room ceiling using brackets I had made some time ago.

Dec. 23 • Contractor came and installed roof gutters and down spouts.

• Electricians installed remaining light fixtures.

• Installed weather stripping on basement door.

Dec. 24 • NA

Dec. 25 • Christmas Day. NA

Dec. 26 • Received results of county water test in the mail. Water tested okay.

• Held a housewarming family dinner in the new house. We used the fireplace for the first time and it worked quite well.

Dec. 27   • Plumbing inspector came and gave his approval.
           • Hooked up refrigerator ice-maker rather than ask Greenie to do it.
           • Carpet people came and completed the installation.
Dec. 28   • Prepared for moving day.
Dec. 29   • Sunday. Installed smoke detectors and started moving my shop machines since I prefer not to have the movers do this job.
Dec. 30   • A county inspector came to give inspection for the occupancy permit. He wanted another smoke detector placed in the basement and hand rails installed at the three-step entrance from the garage to the screened porch. Most disturbing, the screened frame and screened door at this same entrance had to be replaced with fire-resistant drywall and a metal door. Later this day I put up the extra smoke detector and the hand rails. He wanted me to call him at eight o'clock the following morning.
Dec. 31   • Called the inspector as requested. He wanted to meet with me regarding the fireproofing at the screened porch door sometime between one and five o'clock in the afternoon. I waited but he never showed.

The Month of January

On the afternoon of January 2nd, the county inspector showed up to discuss the fireproofing. He had talked it over with the chief inspector and as he previously had told me, fireproofing would be required before he would issue an occupancy permit. What he did not know was that earlier in the day we had already moved in. The movers and the truck were gone by the time the inspector showed and I did not bring up the subject — nor did he. Wells had assured me that there would be no problem with the inspector over moving in and he was right. It looked to me like the county could get tough on this subject if they had to, but they do not enforce the letter of the law for minor infractions.

Now my problem was how to get the job of fireproofing done. I could just turn it over to Wells and walk away. Carpenters, drywall installers, and procurement of a door and other materials would be necessary. I reviewed my options and decided that the fastest and least expensive route would be for me to temporarily cancel my other activities and do the job myself. The next day found me purchasing a metal door and fire-rated drywall. I had no problem with the installation and on January 6th I called the inspector's office. To my surprise, I found that the official record showed two items: one that the house had been approved and another that the house had been rejected. Finally I spoke to the inspector himself who said he would straighten out the record.

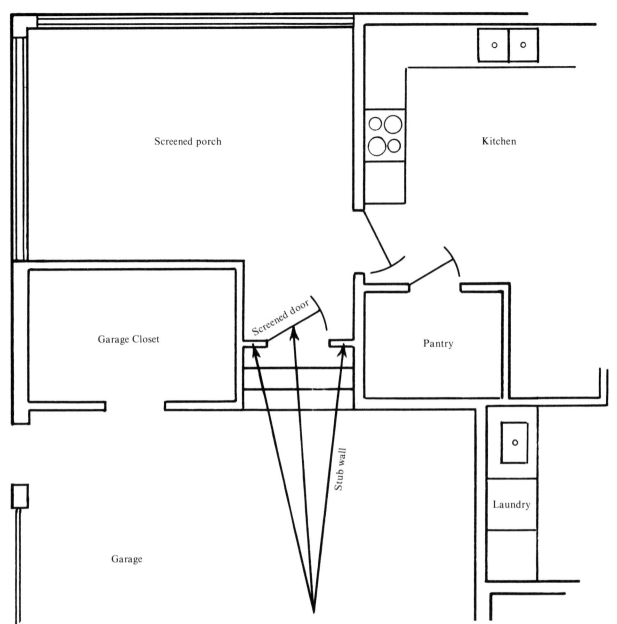

According to county codes, walls common to the house and garage must be faced with fire-rated drywall on the garage side. The drywall installers had done this. In addition, the county inspector insisted that the stub walls indicated also be surfaced with fire-rated drywall and that the screened door be replaced with a fire-rated door.

This time I had to call his appointment office to set a date for him to make the inspection. I did as he told me and made a date for the following day. He did not show. The next day, January 7th, I called and he said he would meet me that day. This time he showed up and verbally approved. He could not, however, read the name of the electrical inspector on one particular approval sticker. He needed this before issuing the occupancy permit. We would have to await his review of the record "back at the office." On the eighth of January, I called the inspector and he said all was okay. He would meet me that afternoon at our house to give approval and to remove the rejection sticker. He did not show. I kept calling, and Hallelujah! he showed and handed us an approved occupancy permit. It was January 13th. I was a little disgusted but happy too.

At this time the house was comfortable but not at all complete in detail. We had, however, moved into the house with a county occupancy permit. Since the bulk of the money had already been spent, I decided that January was a good place to cut off this part of the saga of the house construction. It is picked up again in Chapter VIII, *Moving In, Almost Hooray!*

January, day by day

Jan. 1   •   Happy New Year!

Jan. 2   •   Called the county inspector and he apologized for not showing on Dec. 31st as he said he would. He did come in the afternoon and confirmed that I would have to fireproof the entranceway from the garage to the screened porch.

Jan. 3   •   Decided that the quickest way to get the fireproof door and wall up was to do it myself. I started calling suppliers to locate the materials needed.

Jan. 4   •   Purchased the fireproof door and fire-rated drywall needed for the job.

Jan. 5   •   Sunday. Although the weather was close to freezing, I was able to complete the drywall work, including the joint compound application.

        •   Hung the new metal door.

Jan. 6   •   Called the county inspector and told him I was ready for his final inspection. He said that he had recorded a formal rejection on our house. Therefore, I should make a formal request for inspection through the appointment office, which I did.

        •   Telephone people came to replace the temporary telephone line (which was lying on the ground) with a permanently buried one. They found the ground too muddy to work and said they would be back another day.

Jan. 7   •   Called the county inspector and he said he would be at the house in the afternoon. I waited but he did not show.

Jan. 8   •   Called the county inspector and he said he would make his inspection in the morning. This time he kept his word and after looking things over he verbally approved. He removed the rejection sticker but because he could not read the inspector's name on the electrical approval sticker, he would not issue a formal occupancy permit. After his review of his office record he would send us the formal occupancy permit.

		Telephone people installed permanent buried telephone line.
Jan. 9	•	NA (No Activity)
Jan. 10	•	NA
Jan. 11	•	NA
Jan. 12	•	Sunday. NA
Jan. 13	•	Finally, the inspector drove into our driveway and handed me the occupancy permit.

6

That's The Way The Money Goes

Financial arrangements to pay for this house were relatively simple. Recall that we had sold our previous house and had immediately placed the proceeds, about $300,000, into an interest bearing account. Soon after, I put $100,000 of this into an investment that would provide us income during our retirement years, leaving 200,000 dollars to build the house. How did I arrive at $200,000? I had two independent estimates of the cost to build by competent builders. Both estimates are given in chapter 4. The builder I selected (Wells) estimated a total of $174,050 and the second builder estimated $195,050. Considering that the second builder's fee was $9,000 more than Well's fee, the estimates were quite similar. So I provided a conservative $200,000, but I also saw to it that part of the $100,000, which I had invested for retirement income, could be liquidated and made available to pay for the house just in case there had been a gross miscalculation. The risk associated with *mis-financing* is great and fortunately, I will not be able to give you an actual example for this house. Nevertheless a simple mental projection will confirm that mis-financing indeed brings on great risk. When the money runs out and the first bill goes unpaid the word spreads among the subcontractors very fast. Work on the house soon stops, or if the owner or builder can convince the subcontractors that things are okay, it stops later when the next bill goes unpaid. If the house is being put up with borrowed money, the interest payment on the loan continues and if this can't be paid, there are further financial penalties. In our county, subcontractors have, by law, a limited time during which they can place liens on a house, so soon the sheriff arrives and posts liens on the front door. The next step is a lawyer. Sound like a horror story? Believe that it happens.

A previous house we built suffered a different fate from the present house. I had a contract with a good builder who had a fine local reputation. He was finishing a number of houses and also had just started to build four other houses for local buyers, some of whom I knew. I felt quite secure in the fact that under my contract the builder had to supply me with a receipt signed by the subcontractor or supplier, for each payment made on my house over $300. When the house approached completion I had a lot of signed receipts but that did not stop the sheriff from posting lien notices on my front door. I told the sheriff that I had signed receipts from each of those subcontractors who were placing liens. He said, "Just doin' my job" and walked away. I was furious. I stormed into the mason's office (one of the largest liens was from them) and demanded to see the boss. He did not want to talk to me. I waited and made myself annoying enough that the boss finally said, "Okay, but only for a minute." I showed him the signed receipts on *his stationery*. He said, "That's not my signature and we have not been paid." He glared at the receipt on his own stationery for a moment, then sailed it through the air back at me. The conversation had ended. I called the other owners for whom my builder was building. They were in trouble too. I called a lawyer and he looked into it. My receipts had all been forged. Some time later the lawyer, the five owners, and the builder all met at the lawyer's office. The builder had lost his house, car, trucks, and most things he owned of value. He had a wife and children and I could not help feel some compassion for his family. Surely he had not intended for things to end this way. The liens got partially paid off and each owner received a note for the balance signed by the builder, which was obviously worthless. Well, not exactly worthless; we could deduct our notes from our income taxes as bad debts. Not a pleasant trip for him *or* us. As the builder left the office he slammed the door, then an instant later he abruptly opened it and thrust only his head into the office. He said, "You know, if this deal were over a few million dollars you wouldn't be talking to me this way." Slammmmmm. The story goes on but enough has been said.

Perhaps it is now evident why I felt more secure under my arrangement with Wells where I paid the bills personally. Yes, it is more work but it is also more secure. Wells probably felt safer too, not having to make payments with other people's money. There was still a little room for hanky-panky, but not much, and it is better than other arrangements I've seen.

Following is a log of expenditures made during building. It carries from inception, January 10, 1985, through February 6, 1986, the period when the bulk of the bills to construct the house was incurred and paid. We moved into the house January 2, 1986, so you see we were still paying bills for a time after moving in.

LOG OF EXPENDITURES TO BUILD HOUSE

	PAID TO/PURPOSE	HOW PAID	DATE BILL PAID	AMOUNT
Initial Expenditures through the month of March $243.58	Drafting Supply Co./Tracing paper, drafting supplies	Cash	1-10-85	$40^{00}
	Copy Service Co./Blueprints of house drawings	Cash	2-8-85	12^{00}
	Copy Service Co./Blueprints of house drawings	Cash	3-14-85	25^{58}
	Electric Power Co./Hook-up fee	CK	3-19-85	166^{00}
Expenditures For April $1,575.56	County/Partial building permit	CK	4-1-85	$165^{56}
	County/Well permit	CK	4-1-85	35^{00}
	Surveyor/Set building stakes	CK	4-1-85	375^{00}
	County/Environmental deposit*	CK	4-15-85	1,000^{00}
Expenditures For May $13,758.86	Builder's Fee/Pmt. 1 (500/week)	CK	5-2-85	$500^{00}
	Builder's Fee/Pmt. 2	CK	5-2-85	500^{00}
	County/Building permit final	CK	5-2-85	97^{00}
	Electrician/Install temporary power	CK	5-3-85	125^{00}
	Builder's Fee/Pmt. 3	CK	5-6-85	500^{00}
	Building Supply Co./Metal door frames	CK	5-8-85	235^{00}

*Refundable when lawn is established

PAID TO/PURPOSE	HOW PAID	DATE BILL PAID	AMOUNT
Mason/ Footing layout & supervision, advance on first draw	CK	5-10-85	5,000.00
Bulldozer Service/ Excavate, dig footings	CK	5-10-85	400.00
Concrete Co./ Concrete for footings	CK	5-10-85	1,464.06
Builder's Fee/ Pmt. 4	CK	5-12-85	500.00
Builder's Fee/ Pmt. 5	CK	5-20-85	500.00
Building Supply Co./ Metal trusses, decking for screened porch	CK	5-22-85	644.80
Builder's Fee/ Pmt. 6	CK	5-27-85	500.00
Carpenter/ First draw (Subflooring)	CK	5-29-85	2,793.00
Builder's Fee/ Pmt. 7	CK	6-2-85	$500.00
Portable Toilet Co./ (62.40 per mo.)	CK	6-2-85	62.40
Lumber Yard/ Lumber, plywood	CK	6-2-85	6,445.41
Coating Co./ Spray asphalt coating on foundation walls	CK	6-4-85	100.00
Bobcat Service/ Place and spread basement gravel	CK	6-4-85	250.00
Mason/ Balance on first draw	CK	6-6-85	9,464.00
Gravel Supply Co./ Finish gravel for bsmt.	CK	6-6-85	443.30
Builder's Fee/ Pmt. 8	CK	6-10-85	500.00
Copy Service Co./ Blueprints of house drawings	CK	6-11-85	12.00
Hardware Store/ Masonry paint	CK	6-15-85	200.96
Kitchen Supply House/ Partial pmt. kitchen cabinets	CK	6-18-85	1,348.09
Plumber/ First draw (Plumbing in ground)	CK	6-19-85	3,000.00
Concrete Finisher/ Finish basement slab, wire mesh	CK	6-19-85	1,303.00
Builder's Fee/ Pmt. 9	CK	6-20-85	500.00
Carpenter/ Second draw (Framing)	CK	6-20-85	2,534.95
Builder's Fee/ Pmt. 10	CK	6-24-85	500.00

Expenditures for June 33,579.76

PAID TO/PURPOSE	HOW PAID	DATE BILL PAID	AMOUNT
Window Supply Co./ Windows for house	CK	6-24-85	4,896.22
Kitchen Supply House/ Bathtub and fixtures	CK	6-27-85	957.03
Portable Toilet Co.	CK	6-30-85	62.40
Builder's Fee/ Pmt. 11	CK	6-30-85	500.00
Expenditures for July 18,165.43 — Roof Truss Supplier/ Roof trusses	CK	7-3-85	$2,892.41
Concrete Co./ Basement floor	CK	7-3-85	1,834.37
Building Supply Co./ Steel beams	CK	7-3-85	1,204.48
Lumber Yard/ Lumber	CK	7-5-85	2,501.43
Builder's Fee/ Pmt. 12	CK	7-6-85	500.00
Builder's Fee/ Pmt. 13	CK	7-14-85	500.00
Carpenter/ Third draw (Roof)	CK	7-18-85	3,874.50
Trucking Service/ Deliver fill dirt	CK	7-18-85	144.70
Roofing Co./ First draw (Paper roof)	CK	7-18-85	396.00
Electrician/ Install temporary power addition	CK	7-19-85	150.00
Builder's Fee/ Pmt 14	CK	7-21-85	500.00
Electrician/ Furnish, install attic fan	VISA	7-23-85	150.00
Hardware Store/ Wire for stereo	VISA	7-23-85	6.54
Lumber Yard/ Wood for stereo speaker brackets	Cash	7-26-85	11.00
Builder's Fee/ Pmt. 15	CK	7-23-85	500.00
Electrician/ First draw (Rough-in)	CK	7-30-85	3,000.00
Expenditures for August 24,353.24 — Hardware Store/ Misc. hardware	VISA	8-1-85	$50.90
Building Supply Co./ Angle iron	Cash	8-2-85	19.35
Builder's Fee/ Pmt. 16	CK	8-5-85	500.00
Lumber Yard/ Lumber, plywood	CK	8-5-85	472.71
Electric Power Co./ Electricity used	CK	8-5-85	17.05
Portable Toilet Co.	CK	8-5-85	62.40

PAID TO/PURPOSE	HOW PAID	DATE BILL PAID	AMOUNT
Hardware Store / Rosin paper and tacks	VISA	8-6-85	9.13
Building Supply Co. / Concrete re-enforcement rod	CK	8-8-85	22.88
Concrete Finisher / Finish garage, porch	CK	8-9-85	763.50
Kitchen Supply House / Part payment bathroom cabinets	CK	8-9-85	557.78
Builder's Fee / Pmt. 17	CK	8-12-85	500.00
Hardware Store / Chimney caps	VISA	8-12-85	56.13
Electronic Supply Shop / TV antenna	VISA	8-12-85	38.07
Electronic Supply Shop / Antenna supplies	VISA	8-13-85	12.44
Hardware Store / Flashing, electric boxes	VISA	8-14-85	17.20
Hardware Store / Specialty nails	VISA	8-14-85	21.88
Mason / Second draw (Brick veneer & fireplace)	CK	8-16-85	8,277.00
Engineering Services / Test ground density	CK	8-16-85	64.00
Bobcat Service / Grade dirt, gravel at garage	CK	8-16-85	250.00
Concrete / For garage and porch	CK	8-16-85	994.26
Electric Power Co. / Install underground service	CK	8-24-85	189.00
Stair Co. / Provide staircase	CK	8-26-85	203.84
Builder's Fee / Pmt. 18	CK	8-27-85	500.00
Builder's Fee / Pmt. 19	CK	8-27-85	500.00
Well Drilling Co. / Drill Well	CK	8-27-85	1,760.00
Roofers / Second draw (shingle roof)	CK	8-27-85	3,280.00
Portable Toilet Co.	CK	8-29-85	62.40
Insulation Co. / Batt wall insulation	CK	8-31-85	784.00
Heating/AC Co. / First draw (Duct rough-in)	CK	8-31-85	3852.00
Hardware Store / Misc. electrical supplies	CK	8-31-85	4.20
Electric Power Co. / Electricity used	CK	8-31-85	11.12
Builder's Fee / Pmt. 20	CK	8-31-85	500.00

PAID TO/PURPOSE	HOW PAID	DATE BILL PAID	AMOUNT
Expenditures for September 17,583.47			
Insulation Co./Air seal house	CK	9-5-85	$325.00
Septic Tank/Install septic tank & field	CK	9-5-85	4,300.00
Hardware Store/Window installation bolts	Cash	9-6-85	1.62
Hardware Store/Misc. electrical supplies	Cash	9-6-85	2.16
Drywall Co./First Draw (Drywall)	CK	9-6-85	6,000.00
Builder's Fee/Pmt. 21	CK	9-9-85	500.00
Department Store/Ceiling fan	VISA	9-9-85	65.72
Hardware Store/Concrete paint, TV rail	VISA	9-13-85	13.98
Builder's Fee/Pmt. 22	CK	9-14-85	500.00
Lumberyard/Wood for TV installation	CK	8-31-85	12.37
Building Supply Co./Metal doors	CK	9-16-85	926.10
Kitchen Supply House/Balance of payments on kitchen cabinets	CK	9-16-85	2,683.40
Builder's Fee/Pmt. 23	CK	9-23-85	500.00
Electrician/Second draw (Switch & plug)	CK	9-24-85	1,000.00
Paint Store/Paint wall primer	CK	9-24-85	122.08
Paint Store/Paint wall primer	VISA	9-26-85	54.04
Hardware Store/Morter mix	Cash	9-28-85	8.50
Builder's Fee/Pmt. 24	CK	9-30-85	500.00
Building Supply Co./Metal door hinges	CK	9-30-85	56.56
Electric Power Co./Electricity used	CK	9-30-85	11.94
Expenditures for October 10,665.73			
Building Supply Co./Concrete reinforcing rod	CK	10-1-85	$523.35
Drywall Co./Final draw (Drywall)	CK	10-1-85	2,120.00
Hardware Store/Door chimes	VISA	10-1-85	46.77
Tile Store/Sample window sill tile	Cash	10-2-85	1.04
Paint Store/Wall primer paint	CK	10-2-85	43.12

PAID TO/PURPOSE	HOW PAID	DATE BILL PAID	AMOUNT
Portable Toilet Co.	CK	10-5-85	62^{40}
Lumberyard/Lumber and plywood	CK	10-5-85	2,087^{77}
Bulldozer Service/Back fill & grade around house	CK	10-6-85	446^{00}
Central Vacuum Co./Rough-in central vacuum	CK	10-6-85	300^{00}
Well Pump Co./Install well pump, controls	CK	10-6-85	1,450^{00}
Builder's Fee/Pmt. 25	CK	10-6-85	500^{00}
Paint Store/Interior paint/stain	VISA	10-7-85	45^{71}
Lumberyard/Shelving	VISA	10-12-85	31^{46}
Builder's Fee/Pmt. 26	CK	10-15-85	500^{00}
Truck Rentals/Truck for trash clean up	CK	10-15-85	127^{82}
County Dump/Fee for dumping trash	Cash	10-15-85	30^{00}
Builder's Fee/Pmt. 27	CK	10-21-85	500^{00}
Hardware Store/Nails	Cash	10-22-85	3^{63}
Appliance Store/Hood-microwave unit	CK	10-2-85	384^{68}
Kitchen Supply House/Sink and formica counter top	CK	10-23-85	707^{69}
Builder's Fee/Pmt. 28	CK	10-28-85	500^{00}
Electric Power Co./Electricity used	CK	10-28-85	11^{12}
Building Supply Co./Clothes rod supports and hangers	CK	10-28-85	33^{92}
Farm Supply Store/Grass seed and straw	VISA	10-29-85	209^{25}
Carpet Supply Co./First draw (Carpet)	CK	11-4-85	$1,858^{95}
Carpet Supply Co./First draw (Kitchen vinyl flooring)	CK	11-4-85	375^{00}
Builder's Fee/Pmt. 29	CK	11-4-85	500^{00}
Kitchen Supply House/Bathroom counter tops	CK	11-4-85	600^{00}
Hardware Store/Sandpaper	Cash	11-6-85	3^{11}
Lumberyard/Plywood siding and batens	CK	11-6-85	3,176^{23}
Builder's Fee/Pmt. 30	CK	11-11-85	500^{00}

Expenditures
for November
19,612.85

PAID TO/PURPOSE	HOW PAID	DATE BILL PAID	AMOUNT
Lumberyard / Gable triangular vents	VISA	11-11-85	94^{64}
Stone Quarry / Front door stepping stones	CK	11-14-85	92^{61}
Paint Store / Interior paint	Cash	11-15-85	18^{71}
Builder's Fee / Pmt. 31	CK	11-17-85	500^{00}
Carpenter / Fouth draw (Interior trim)	CK	11-20-85	$2,875^{50}$
Hardware Store / Shower door, fireplace tools	VISA	11-20-85	127^{55}
Lumberyard / Trim, lock, hinges, misc.	VISA	11-20-85	47^{33}
Hardware Store / Interior paint	VISA	11-20-85	17^{67}
Hardware Store / Screening for porch	VISA	11-21-85	62^{35}
Building Supply Co. / Door hardware	CK	11-21-85	437^{89}
Hardware Store / Interior house paint	VISA	11-22-85	27^{71}
Builder's Fee / Pmt. 32 (Final pmt.)	CK	11-26-85	500^{00}
Plumber / Second draw	CK	11-26-85	$5,500^{00}$
Insulation Co. / Blow in attic insulation	CK	11-27-85	864^{00}
Kitchen Supply House / Appliances: stove, refrigerator, dishwasher	CK	11-27-85	$1,403^{44}$
Hardware Store / Fireplace grate	VISA	11-27-85	30^{16}
Light Fixtures Co. / Part payment on light fixtures	CK	12-3-85	$\$548^{71}$
Lumberyard / Plywood siding, redwood for porch	CK	12-7-85	$1,112^{77}$
Hardware Store / Interior paint	Cash	12-9-85	2^{90}
Heating / AC Co. / Second draw	CK	12-10-85	$2,568^{00}$
Garage Door Co. / Install door, opener	CK	12-10-85	814^{00}
Bulldozer Service / Furnish gravel, final rough grading	CK	12-10-85	$1,819^{90}$
Carpenter / Fifth draw (Exterior siding)	CK	12-10-85	$3,400^{00}$
Electric Power Co. / Electricity used	CK	12-10-85	11^{12}
Hardware Store / Shelf hardware	Cash	12-10-85	3^{52}
Masonry Supply Store / Chimney thimble	Cash	12-10-85	2^{60}

Expenditures for December 15,865.86

PAID TO/PURPOSE	HOW PAID	DATE BILL PAID	AMOUNT
Iron Works/ Front door railings	Cash	12-10-85	160.00
Carpet Supply Co./ Final draw (Kitchen vinyl flooring)	CK	12-10-85	381.25
Hardware Store/ Light fixtures misc.	VISA	12-13-85	10.35
Light Fixtures Co./ Part payment on light fixtures	CK	12-18-85	35.36
Hardware Store/ Light fixtures misc.	VISA	12-18-85	15.78
Hardware Store/ Door weather stripping	VISA	12-18-85	20.72
Hardware Store/ Floodlight fixtures	VISA	12-18-85	15.28
Ceramic Tile Co./ Install entrance foyer	CK	12-20-85	994.30
Hardware Store/ Floodlight fixtures	VISA	12-21-85	72.66
Hardware Store/ Electric floodlight bulbs	VISA	12-24-85	10.40
Seamless Gutters Co./ Roof gutters and downspouts	CK	12-27-85	733.00
Hardware Store/ Refrigerator icemaker installation kit	VISA	12-27-85	8.10
Hardware Store/ Misc. hardware	VISA	12-27-85	16.71
Hardware Store/ Smoke detectors	VISA	12-30-85	14.17
Hardware Store/ Plastic sheeting	VISA	12-31-85	8.31
Carpet Supply Co./ Carpeting, final payment	CK	12-31-85	1,858.95
Electrician/ Final payment	CK	12-31-85	1,227.00
Hardware Store/ Closet hooks	VISA	1-4-86	$15.82
Building Supply Co./ Fire-rated drywall	VISA	1-4-86	32.97
Hardware Store/ Drywall corner bead, shower curtain rod	VISA	1-5-86	16.22
Hardware Store/ Bathroom drawer pulls	Cash	1-7-86	6.14
Foam Rubber Store/ Foam rubber for fireplace seats	VISA	1-11-86	76.12
Plumber/ Final payment	CK	1-13-86	1,236.00
County Dump/ Fee for dumping trash	Cash	1-15-86	20.00

Expenditures
for January
3,577.65

PAID TO/PURPOSE	HOW PAID	DATE BILL PAID	AMOUNT
Hardware Store/Tile grout, caulking, paint	VISA	1-21-86	53.88
Mason/Final payment	CK	1-22-86	1,259.00
Hardware Store/Bathroom towel racks, paper holders	VISA	1-24-86	61.50
Carpenter/Final payment	CK	1-24-86	800.00
Hardware Store/Folding door for laundry	VISA	2-2-86	$155.59
Central Vacuum Co./Final payment for central vacuum	CK	2-6-86	535.00
TOTAL Expenditures through February 6			**159,672.58**

Expenditures for February through Feb. 6 690.59

Once moved in, payments quickly stretched out like switching from normal speed to slow motion on a VCR. After all, the emphasis instantly switched from getting things finished to making everything work. To complete the financial picture on the house subsequent to the arbitrary Feb. 6 cut-off date, there were two types of expenditures, actual and estimated. Following are tables of these expenditures.

EXPENDITURES AFTER CUT OFF DATE OF FEBRUARY 6

PAID TO/PURPOSE	HOW PAID	DATE BILL PAID	AMOUNT
Sears/Water filter	Acct.	3-6-86	$50.45
Musser Forests/Landscape plants	CK	3-13-86	247.87
Electric Fixture Supplier/Light fixtures	CK	3-21-86	340.00
Paint Store/Outside house paint	VISA	3-21-86	93.77
Paint Store/Garage floor sealer	VISA	4-4-86	28.05
Building Supply House/Drain pipe	CK	4-4-86	63.76
Nursery Supply House/Railroad ties	CK	4-5-86	199.51
Hardware Store/Sacrete	VISA	4-10-86	5.30
Nursery Supply House/Alberta spruce trees	Cash	4-18-86	20.76

PAID TO/PURPOSE	HOW PAID	DATE BILL PAID	AMOUNT
Quarry Supplies / Driveway gravel	CK	5-15-86	452^{76}
Nearby Builder / Fill dirt	CK	5-16-86	150^{00}
Nursery Supply House / Grass seed & fertilizer	VISA	5-17-86	128^{98}
Hardware Store / Hose hangers	Cash	5-17-86	6^{22}
Hardware Store / Window blinds, clothesline reel, treated clothesline post	Cash	5-17-86	131^{50}
Nursery Supply House / Maple tree	Cash	5-21-86	20^{71}
Nursery Supply House / Garden timber	Cash	5-26-86	5^{20}
Nursery Supply House / Split rail fence	VISA	6-02-86	96^{15}
Hardware Store / Wood preservative	VISA	6-08-86	19^{88}
Building Supply House / Down spout fittings	Cash	8-26-86	16^{71}
Nursery Supply House / Grass seed	VISA	9-02-86	49^{90}
Lumberyard / Step for outside	Cash	9-11-86	11^{23}
Hardware Store / Paint, bifold door	VISA	10-28-86	88^{37}
Hardware Store / Caulking for windows	Cash	11-24-86	6^{41}
TOTAL Expenditures after February 6			2,233^{49}

ESTIMATE OF ADDITIONAL EXPENDITURES TO COMPLETE HOUSE

Complete interior decoration	$1,700^{00}
Tile basement floor	2,000^{00}
Windowsill tile and supplies	200^{00}
Gravel, dress up driveway	300^{00}
Complete the planting around house	300^{00}
TOTAL	4,500^{00}
County refund of environmental deposit	-1,000^{00}
TOTAL Estimated expenditures	3,500^{00}

SUMMARY OF HOUSE EXPENDITURES

Expenditures from inception through February 6	$159,672^{58}$
Expenditures after February 6	$2{,}233^{49}$
Estimated additional expenditures to complete house	$3{,}500^{00}$
TOTAL cost to construct house	$165{,}406^{07}$

Here is a chart that shows *when*, month by month, money was needed during construction.

MONTH	MONTHLY EXPENDITURES	CUMULATIVE EXPENDITURES
Through March	243^{58}	243^{58}
April	$1{,}575^{56}$	$1{,}819^{14}$
May	$13{,}758^{86}$	$15{,}578^{00}$
June	$33{,}579^{76}$	$49{,}157^{76}$
July	$18{,}165^{43}$	$67{,}323^{19}$
August	$24{,}353^{24}$	$91{,}676^{43}$
September	$17{,}583^{47}$	$109{,}259^{90}$
October	$10{,}665^{73}$	$119{,}925^{63}$
November	$19{,}612^{85}$	$139{,}538^{48}$
December	$15{,}865^{86}$	$155{,}404^{34}$
January	$3{,}577^{65}$	$158{,}981^{99}$
February (through Feb. 6) Actual and Estimated	690^{69}	$159{,}981^{88}$
Cost after Feb. 6	573^{99}	$165{,}406^{07}$

In the opening chapter I explained that I had financial goals and that a key to achieving these was the cost of constructing the house. My financial goal for constructing the house was $150,000. The actual cost ended up to be $165,406.07 (love that seven cents) and this exceeds the goal by a shade over ten percent. Although we did not bull's-eye the target we did beat Wells' estimate by $8,644. I like to think that my efforts and Wells' cooperation made the difference. Perhaps if I had not set a financial goal (and tried to meet it) the costs would have amounted to a lot more. Following is a graph which summarizes much of what has been said above — take a good look at it. I'm satisfied that we achieved the lion's share of the financial goal which is, in the end, only a part of a dream house.

EXPENDITURES VS. MONTHS

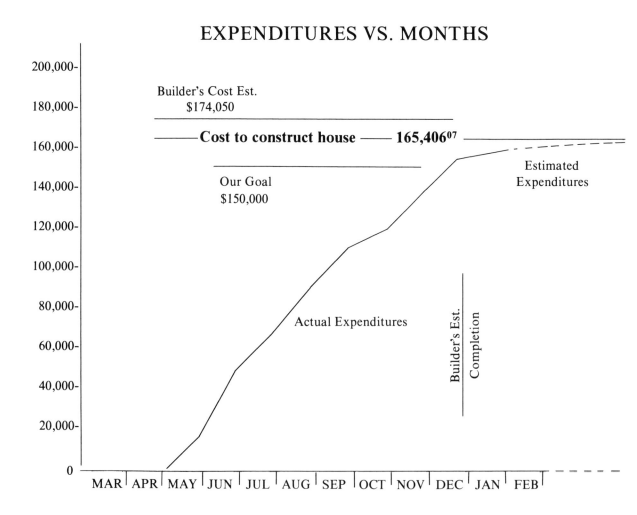

Before we started to build, I often wished I had access to a chronological list of expenses such as the one above. By summing up all payments to the carpenter, one can tell the total cost for carpentry. In this case, it was close to the carpenter's actual contract bid. Total cost for plumbing, drywall, electrical and builder's fees, etc. can be similarly determined. In the same manner, the cost of many materials such as windows and lumber can be established. Should another house of similar style be under consideration, the values can be percentaged up or down accordingly. An actual window count from one house (see the house plans given in chapter 3) can be compared to another house and from this an equivalent estimate of window costs can be derived. For some items, values can be reduced to dollars per square foot and then applied to another house plan. As time goes on it may seem that the values given in the chart will change so that after a few years, they will be less valid. This, of course, will be true to some extent, but my experience has been that the balance between values will change little for years to come. For example, I expect a percentage change reflecting inflation, either up or down, to be quite valid for many years. Building costs in the Northern Virginia area (near Washington DC where our house was built) are undoubtedly higher than many other areas in the country. In a similar manner, the costs can be percentaged to reflect your local conditions.

How do you start the cost analysis for your dream house? Go to the neighborhood where you want to build and get the price the builder is asking for a house similar to what you want. If this is not practical, then pick a fairly new house which is for sale or which sold recently and get the sale price. Any responsible real estate sales person can obtain the price for you. If you think you want to buy a lot in the area, the sales person will be more than glad to get you the price of the house (and the lot too). Ask for a plat showing the house dimensions. If none is available, pace the outside dimensions of the house and make your own sketch. With a little more pencil work, you will have the square footage of the house plan. Your dream house will be a little bigger or smaller, so proportion the figures accordingly and make corrections for known differences. If you continue your efforts, you will soon have a peek at what a builder's estimate will look like.

Don't be afraid to make estimates on your own. Estimates never hit the nail on the head, but they are always useful for guidance. I would have felt better if I'd had a detailed cost guide to use in paying the bills just to be able to assess whether or not my payments were reasonable. As it was, when I was unsure about a payment, I would turn to Wells and say, "Does this bill look reasonable to you?" and he would always give some sort of guidance.

COMBINED COST OF HOUSE AND LOT:

Cost of lot (from chapter 2)	52,067^{99}
Cost to construct house	165,406^{07}
Total cost of lot and house	217,474^{06}

7

Subcontractor and Supplier Contracts

The array of different bids and contracts was dazzling and only the most important ones are discussed here. I had planned to reproduce the actual bids/contracts just as I had received them. Many of them were handwritten and proved to be difficult or impossible to read. So the decision was made to tidy each one into an intelligible form. I have, however, held closely to the original formats although names and addresses have been deleted or changed. Where bids/contracts were handwritten I have reproduced them in handwriting. The five biggest dollar-eaters for our particular house, when totaled, comprised 51% of the construction cost. I list them up front to establish a sense of perspective.

1. Masonry		$24,000
2. Carpentry		16,278
3. Builder's Fee		16,000
4. Lumberyard		15,991
5. Plumbing		9,736

Masonry

The mason won the largest share. He furnished all masonry materials and labor under a fixed-price contract. The specialty materials and county codes make it too complicated for the owner/builder to furnish materials separately. Bill, the head mason, did everything. He signed, negotiated, laid brick and blocks — just about everything. "I like your house," he said, "I'm going to do the same thing for myself and my wife as soon as my youngest is out of college — in about three years." He was not a young man and I marveled at how he could handle the large heavy concrete blocks all day long. Like many of the other subcontractors, his was a low overhead operation in the extreme. You will remember that I was annoyed with Wells because he asked me to make a payment to Bill before I had seen Bill's bid on paper. In retrospect, I believe that Bill never intended to furnish one. He had given a verbal quote and that was enough for him. I persisted, however, and got my way. Below is the neatened up version of Bill's contract. The only written record of our agreement to reduce the price to $24,000 is my notation at the lower center which I made while talking to Bill on the phone.

MASONRY CONTRACT

TO: *Charles Daniels*

FROM: *Bill*

MESSAGE

Contract as per plan includes extra block in garage and extra two courses of block in foundation.

Brick allowance $180^{00} per thousand	$25,723^{00}
Draw schedule	
1. When basement is completed	$14,464^{00}
2. When fireplace and brick veneer is completed	$10,000^{00}
3. When porch top and steps and washdown of brick is completed.	$1,259^{00}
TOTAL	$25,723^{00}

Now 24000 Tele. discussion July 13, 85

116

Note that Bill calls out two extra courses of block in the foundation which was not true. The house plans were the same before as after he bid and there were no extra block courses required. The plans called for a full height eight foot ceiling downstairs. Perhaps Bill was used to something less than that, so in his view it required an extra two courses of block. At Wells' suggestion we did add a foundation wall across the automobile entrance to the garage. This did add extra blocks and it is noted in the bid.

Bill calls for "draws" in his contract. This is a common practice. Here he starts the work with his own money and when he reaches a certain stage of progress he calls for the first payment, or draw. This process is a sort of safety net for the owner/builder and avoids advancing money for work not yet done. Bill also resorts to the allowance, another common practice. Note that his allowance for bricks was $180 per thousand. The bricks we specified cost less than that but it was a small amount and I never spoke to Bill about it. I have, of course, signed receipts for each payment made for the entire house, but they are far too numerous to show and I have not reproduced them here.

The masonry crew consisted of three or four men depending on the demands of the day. Before we leave Bill and his crew, I must tell you about Charles, a strong middle-aged black fellow who did most of the mortar mixing. Black does not describe his skin — it really was ebony purple and it glistened when the sun shone on it. He had a delightful Barbadian accent, an accent I remembered from my earlier days in Panama. "Did you come from the islands?" I asked him. "No, but my mother and father did," he replied. Charles sang a lot, many times religious songs. "Hello, Mr. Wells, I'm glad to see you lookin' so fine. I'm glad you still with us after that accident you had. I loves you Wells! I'm *glad* to see you still with us!" "Charles, you know you don't mean a word of that," said Wells. "I really do, Wells, though sometimes you make me want to say somethin' else." This friendly banter went on day after day and is still going on out there somewhere.

Carpentry

The number two dollar-eater was the carpentry contract. Until I talked with Binney, I was not confident that many of the details of construction would get done. The range of jobs is so wide it would take a wordy contract indeed to cover them all. For a one page fixed-price contract, which is reproduced below, Binney did quite well. The carpenters did not furnish any of the lumber and this was both good and bad. Because lumber and other materials were frequently lacking, it left carpenters stranded on the job with no work to do. On the other hand, Wells and I had the say over the lumberyard orders, and thereby had some control over plywood and lumber overages which always turned into

117

waste. Carpentry was a fixed-price contract, and perhaps if we had asked Binney to also furnish the lumber it would have saved money. Then again, Binney may not have wanted to accept the responsibility. We will never know.

The carpenters undertook many different activities. Here is a list of some of the things they installed: floor joists and subflooring, wall framing both interior and exterior, exterior sheathing, roof trusses, roof sheathing, furring in basement, interior and exterior doors, door hardware, windows, stairs in the stairwell, bannister, kitchen cabinets, underlayments for vinyl and tile floors, shelves, interior trim, closet hardware, screened porch frames and screening, outside siding and vertical battens, and outside trim. They also made framing changes where required by heating and air conditioning people. The different kinds of fasteners, usually nails and screws, also comprise a long list. The carpenters furnished all fasteners which seemed the only practical approach.

House carpentry is a relatively dangerous trade especially for newcomers. Someone in the crew, and this could vary from one to ten carpenters, always had some minor injury. Binney's company was partly a family business; he had a brother who did most of the company's paperwork, but who also doubled as a carpenter when the demand required. One day, while framing another house, Binney's brother fell and broke his leg. Seemingly, this would not affect the construction of our house. It did, however, because it drew Binney off his normal job of foreman in order to do paperwork. He also had to double up for his brother's lost carpentry. Wells said, "Yea, not a very efficient arrangement since Binney isn't as good at the paperwork."

During the early construction of the house, we decided to leave the downstairs rooms unfinished. However, Binney had early on given his bid for completion of the whole house. I asked him to put up the studs for partitions but to leave it at that. He was to deduct something for the remaining unneeded work on one of his draws, which he did. The total on his quotation is therefore slightly different from the actual amount paid. Our agreements were handled verbally without paperwork. Here is the final accounting.

Contract price	$16,454^{00}
Power generator rented by carpenter	+98^{95}
	16,552^{95}
Unfinished downstairs credit	-275^{00}
Total payments	16,277^{95}

CARPENTRY CONTRACT

Proposal submitted to: Charles J. Daniels

Architects: C.J. Daniels   Job site: Daniels Res.

We hereby submit specifications and estimates for:

> Labor only to complete all carpentry work - rough framing and trim as outlined per scope of work.
> Placement of steel beams, floor joist and sub-sheathing, ext. and int. wood partitions, roof truss, conventional rafters, roof sheathing, back-up blocking behind subcontractors, window and door units, ext. trim, int. trim, screened porch.

> Scope of work not to include:
> concrete form work, fences, hardwood floors, roofing.

> Carpenters to provide all rough framing hardware - nails, etc.

> Owner to provide lumber millwork, and elect. on site.

Draw schedule:		
	1st floor deck	2,793 00
	Roof	4,305 00
	Framing	2,436 00
	Ext. trim, siding	3,400 00
	Int. trim	2,720 00
	Final	800 00
	Total	16,454 00

We propose hereby to furnish material and labor -complete in accordance with above specifications, for the sum of:

Sixteen thousand four hundred fifty four and 00/00 dollars ($16,454)

Payment to made as follows: As per draw schedule. Draws to be paid seven days upon receipt of billing.

Authorized signature _Binney_

Note: This proposal may be withdrawn by us if not accepted within 45 days.

119

Plumbing

Fifth in the dollar-eater parade was plumbing. Greenie had a formal business going with work crews, a store house, an office, and trucks. His contract was essentially fixed-price, and he furnished all materials and labor. The one exception to this work was the master bathroom bathtub. You will notice that he made an allowance of $1,500 on the bathtub and we found and furnished a tub costing less than this. He also said his bid was based on the gas line and water line entering the house where he verbally requested. Accordingly he wanted extra payment when it became necessary to change from his recommendations. As it ended, we paid $9,736 on Greenie's contract. We paid a separate $957 for the tub, spout, handgrips, and drain, bringing our plumbing costs to a total of $10,558. Greenie's original bid, including the $1,500 tub allowance was $10,866. After all that, we had reduced our plumbing costs $173 below Greenie's original bid. I guess we won but I'm not sure.

It was important to Greenie to be in charge. He wanted to be king of the hill and he ran his show that way. Among others, he had two easy going, hard working sons in his crew. Greenie's two page contract which clearly calls out three draws follows. When I mailed the final payment to Greenie I included a note "Thanks for a good job."

PLUMBING CONTRACT

Page 1 of 2 Pages

Proposal submitted to
Charles J. Daniels and Wells

We hereby submit specifications and estimates for:

Necessary material and labor to waste, vent, water pipe and set fixtures as per plans and specifications. Groundworks, waste, vents, to be Schedule 40 PVC plastic pipe; Water piping to be Type M copper.

Basement Bath:
Rough in only, water closet, vanity, tub 5'
1-3" floor drain
1-50 gallon gas 5 year heater
Gas pipe furnace and water heater. (Furnace supplied by others)
3-Hose bibbs

First Floor:
1-kitchen sink connection
1-Moen sink faucet #7533A
1-#333 disposal
1-Dishwasher connection
1-FL TD Double compartment L/T
Rough brass faucet
1-Washer stand pipe box

We propose hereby to furnish material and labor - complete in accordance with above specifications, for the sum of:

TEN THOUSAND EIGHT HUNDRED SIXTY SIX DOLLARS ($10,866.00)

Payment to be made as follows:

Three thousand ($3,000.00) on groundwork; Seven thousand ($7,000) on waste, vent, water pipe; $866.00 on setting of fixtures.

Signature _Greenie_

PLUMBING CONTRACT

Proposal submitted to
Charles J. Daniels and Wells

We hereby submit specifications and estimates for:

Hall Bath:
1-#3500 E.B. white water closet
1-Vanity connection and Moen lav. faucet #4625
1-K 715 cast iron 5' tub - white
1-Moen tub and showervalve #2739 chrome

Master Bath:
1-#K3500 E.B. white water closet
1-Vanity connection
1-Moen lav. faucet #4625
1-4' x 5' shower pan for tile
1-Shower faucet Moen #2720 chrome
1-Fiberglass bathing pool white 72" x 36" x 18"
1-Moen tub valve #2739

Note: This Bathing Pool is $1500.00 allowance.

We propose hereby to furnish material and labor - complete in accordance with above specifications, for the sum of:

_____ DOLLARS ($ _10,866 00_)

Signature _Greenie_

Builder's Fee

The builder's fee came in third. I paid $500 weekly to the builder for thirty-two weeks as verbally agreed upon and recorded in Wells' cost estimate for the house. This subject is covered in Chapter 4, *The Builder And His Bid.*

Lumberyard

Number four was the lumberyard. They furnished a lot more than just the lumber and their real name included "woodworking and lumber." They did supply all the lumber but they also furnished tongue and groove plywood for the subfloor, plywood sheathing for the roof and sides of the house, plywood underlayment for vinyl and tile floors, pre-hung interior and exterior doors, various moldings for trim, exterior plywood siding, solid wood battens, and more. This was a big and formal operation. I had no contract per se, but I did have to establish credit with them. Had I taken a bank loan I'm sure it would have been part of the information they would have required. This was a supply on demand arrangement. Both my name and Wells' were included as persons who could draw on the account. From there on, each order for materials became a separate contract. When an order for materials arrived at the building site, it came with a printed invoice. I liked that because I then had a record of just what had been delivered. At the end of each month, I received a billing from the lumberyard listing all invoices for the month. When the billing matched the invoices I had in hand, I knew I was paying for what I had received. This circumvented the possibility of my paying for materials delivered to someone else's job. The fine print on the back of each monthly billing stated that I could deduct two percent of the amount if I paid by the tenth of the month. I always took the discount.

Wells seemed to know everyone in the local building business. When the time came to order the interior doors, Wells showed up at the house with the lumberyard credit manager. The three of us went over the entire house discussing, listing, and marking (on the floor) the size and hinging of each door. When finished, the lumberyard had the order for the doors we needed, and the carpenters had floor markings as to where each door was to be installed. Another day we went to the lumberyard and met again with the credit manager who showed me catalogs of exterior doors. From these catalogs we picked the front and back doors. Here are the front and back of a typical monthly billing.

LUMBERYARD
(billing)

Charles Daniels

Customer No.
0062050

TRANSACTION DATE	INVOICE NUMBER	TRANSACTION TYPE	INVOICE AMOUNT	PAYMENT AMOUNT
		Balance Forward 3,241.05		
11/29/85	5056841	INVOICE	7.32	
11/21/85	5045571	INVOICE	285.83	
11/18/85	5031401	INVOICE	842.33	
11/08/85		PAYMENT		3241.05

	CURRENT	TOTAL DUE		
	1,135.48	1,135.48		

LUMBERYARD

TERMS OF SALE

ALL ORDERS, SALES AND SHIPMENTS WILL BE ACCEPTED AND EXECUTED BY LUMBERYARD UNDER THE FOLLOWING TERMS AND CONDITIONS:

1. Terms of sale (This paragraph applicable to Lumberyard charge account customers only.) 2% discount will be allowed only if payment of this invoice is received by the 10th of the month following the date of invoice and there are no outstanding past due balances, and is due net the end of the same month and past due thereafter. A finance charge of 1½% per month will be charged on all balances more than 30 days past due until paid.

2. Millwork quotations are net and are not subject to the discount.

3. Shipments shall be inspected upon receipt and if any errors or irregularities exist, they must be reported before use of the merchandise but not later than 5 days after receipt of goods, otherwise no claims or adjustments of any kind will be considered. We assume no responsibility in the use of the merchandise shipped and when placed in work, constitutes acceptance by customer.

123

4. No back charges will be allowed unless approved by Lumberyard in writing.

5. A 15% handling charge will be made on goods returned for credit.

6. Special orders not returnable.

7. In the event this invoice becomes delinquent and Lumberyard engages the services of an attorney to collect the amount due, then subject to the applicable law purchaser and any person jointly and severally liable with the purchaser agrees to reimburse the Lumberyard reasonable legal fees incurred by it whether or not litigation is commenced.

Electrical

Demper was our contractor for electrical work and he had two young West Virginian fellows who did the installing of the electrical wiring, fixtures, etc. They traveled a considerable distance from their homes each morning but always seemed to be on the job early. They joked so much between themselves, I could not tell which one was in charge. Demper would come each day to check on things and give them instructions for the following day. Their closed van was home base for their work and they left it parked on the lot. I knew that they considered their job completed when one day I found the van had departed. Demper's bid was interesting in that it looked like a fixed-price contract. However, it had specific items, such as the number of electrical outlets (light switches and plugs), phone outlets, and recessed outlets (required mostly for closets) which were extra. Demper said that for a house our size the 147 outlets was typical. At the completion of his contract, he made an adjustment for any extra outlets, recessed lights, etc. My appetite for fancy electrical installations is limited but someone else could easily have asked for many costly items. Here Demper had a method of giving an approximate bid and at the same time protecting himself against unusual costs. I would call this a cost-plus-extras contract. Not shown in his bid are the various draws Demper expected. When he asked for a draw, he had already completed a considerable amount of work, and I did not mind making payment. Below is Demper's bid and also his final accounting.

ELECTRICAL CONTRACT

Submitted to: *C. Daniels*

We hereby submit specifications and estimates for:

147 Outlets
400 Amp Circuit Breaker Panel
3 Phone Outlets Complete
2 TV Outlets Wire only
Microwave Oven
Range
Disposal – Dishwasher – Washer-Dryer
Permits – Gas Furnace-Ground Vault
                          Circuit
A/C Wiring – Door Chimes

Fixtures extra   Recessed 43.50 ea
                          complete

We propose hereby to furnish material and labor - complete in accordance with above specifications, for the sum of:

Four thousand seven hundred _dollars ($ 4700 00)

Signature _Demper_

125

ELECTRICAL CONTRACT
(Final billing)

To: Charles Daniels

Contract Price 147 Outlets	4700 00
12 extra outlets @ 18 00	216 00
2 heat lamps 43.50 ea	76 00
4 recessed lights	174 00
220 Circuit for Well	50 00
	5227 00

Payment Rec at Rough-in
3000 00

Plug + Lw 1000 00   4000 00

1227 00

Drywall

Bottle, the drywall contractor, was a pleasant sort of round Dutchman. Wells said he was the most professional of our subcontractors. He had great knowledge of the drywall trade but it is doubtful that he himself was in physical shape to do the work. His crew worked at a remarkably fast pace. It's hard to believe the accuracy they attained cutting, fitting, and applying the drywall sheets. Under this fixed-price contract, Bottle furnished all materials and labor, and his contract calls out three draws. I verbally amended the contract to delete the downstairs rooms and also to place drywall on one wall downstairs to help me control dust from my shop. Bottle's final billing reflected these changes without any paperwork. Here is his one page contract.

DRYWALL CONTRACT

Proposal submitted to
Mr. & Mrs. Daniels

We hereby submit specifications and estimates for:

Drywall: Residence for Mr. & Mrs. Daniels

Basement bedroom, bath, closet and stairway only area to be ½" waterboard to be used in all full baths.

½" firecode board used in garage on ceiling, walls and house side of garage house party wall.

Application to be ½" sheetrock, taped, trowled, sanded and pointed up, ready for paint, using a bead on exposed corners.

We propose hereby to furnish material and labor - complete in accordance with above specifications, for the sum of:

Eight thousand four hundred dollars ($8,400.00). _____

Payment to be made as follows:

65% boarded, 25% taped and trowled, 10% sanded and pointed up.

Signature __*Bottle*_____

Heating and Air Conditioning

We had selected gas forced-hot-air heat with central air conditioning and accepted the bid from the company Wells recommended. I made no attempt to lay out the air ducting but relied on the installers to do the job. There were some minor decisions to be made which we resolved together. When the furnace finally got turned on, I was satisfied with the heating capacity but was disappointed in the noise level. They still have not learned how to make quiet hot air furnaces. This was a fixed-price contract using four draws and a copy of the bid is shown here.

HEATING AND AIR CONDITIONING CONTRACT

To: Wells   **RE: 1 house, rambler residence
for Charles Daniels**

Seller agrees to furnish and install in each of   houses, one
complete forced air system, consisting of all necessary duct work,
with registers and grills, equipment, controls and control wiring,
installed in a neat and workmanlike manner according to standard
practice and plans prepared by seller, each for the sum of: SIXTY
FOUR HUNDRED TWENTY DOLLARS ($6420.00)
Equipment:

Ruud UGDC-07EC 75,000 input, 61,000 output, high efficiency gas
fired furnace 80° plus
Ruud UQB036 condenser 35,500 BTU
Ruud RCAB037 coil
Aprilaire 112 humidifier
Minn Honeywell filter 2000 CFM

Heat and cool first floor, 13 supplies and 2 returns, heat and cool basement, 7
supplies and 1 return, 2 zones with manual control volume dampers.

Items included: control wiring, 2 kitchen exhaust ducts, internal insulation of
return riser, outside air for wood stove, canvas connections
on supply and return plenums, concrete pad for condenser.

Items not included: power wiring, exhaust fans, insulation of ducts not stated.

Purchaser agrees to provide the following items that may be
applicable to this project.

1. All necessary openings required for the installation of ducts
   and flues.
2. Gas furnaces: gas connections to the furnace; a separately
   fused electric circuit within 5' of furnace; A _____ flue crock
   _____ from furnace room floor.
3. Oil furnaces: necessary 230 volt 60 cycle single phase 3 wire
   copper service to furnace as recommended by manufacturer
   of furnace and all local codes, complete with disconnect
   switch where required.
4. Electric furnaces: necessary 230 volt 60 cycle single phase 3
   wire copper service to furnace as recommended by manufacturer of furnace and all local codes, complete with disconnect switch where required.
5. Air conditioning: A 230 volt 60 cycle single phase 3 wire
   copper service for _____ AMPS complete with waterproof
   disconnect switch outside the building for the condensing
   unit or heat pump unit; a concrete slab for outside units; a
   floor drain adjacent to the furnace.

128

6. Water connections to equipment requiring water for its operation.
7. Gas valves external to gas furnace if required and fitting or fitting of humidifier water line to plumbing.

Heating limited warranty: The installation is warranted to maintain 70° F or more in all living rooms of the house when the outside temperature does not go below 0° F. Temperatures of rooms below grade not warranted.

Cooling limited warranty: The installation is warranted to maintain 78° F inside when the outside temperature does not exceed 95° F. inside temperature to be read at thermostat location.

The products to be furnished hereunder, and installation thereof, are limited in warranty to be free from defects in material and workmanship under normal use and maintenance for a period of one year from the date of original installation. This warranty is exclusive and is in lieu of all other warranties, expressed or implied, including any implied or expressed warranty of fitness for a particular application or purpose. The remedies provided for in this warranty are exclusive and shall constitute the only liabilities on part of *Heating & A/c* Co.

It is agreed that: purchaser assumes risk of loss or damage to equipment after installation, seller is not liable for delay caused by strikes, labor difficulties, material or equipment shortages, governmental order or regulations. Any special excise taxes shall be added to purchase price. The prices herein quoted are based on present established prices, and any increase in these prices subsequent to the date of this quotation and prior to the date of installation will be in addition to the above quoted figures. This proposal supersedes any and all previous quotations, agreements and conversations, with reference to this subject, with any member of this organization.

Terms of payment: 15% on roughing in; 45% ducts run back to furnace; 15% furnace hook up; 15% delivery of outside unit; balance on completion of installation, I.E. controls, registers and grilles. Subject to credit approval.

In the event payment is not received by us upon completion, the balance due shall bear interest at 18% per annum until paid. In the event collection of this amount is turned over to our attorney, purchaser agrees to pay attorney's fees of 25% plus all costs associated therewith.

ACCEPTED BY: *Heating and A/c Co.*
PURCHASER: *Charles J. Daniels*
DATE:

Septic Tank and Drain Field

The septic tank and drain field were to be furnished by a local contractor who lived nearby - I suspect he had lived there all his life. His life style and home were less than modest, but his equipment parked throughout the acreage about his house, was

129

superb. His one page fixed-price contract was handwritten but I suspect not by him. Hiding under his appearance and congenial manner was a wealth of experience and knowledge of what could and could not be done in the county. He is almost a one man operation and runs his machines with considerable skill. He did work, such as digging footings, without contract, mostly upon the verbal request of Wells. While doing this septic tank-drain field job, we needed some dirt moved and graded around the well. Also I asked for a couple of scoops of top soil to be placed by my garden for future use. When his final bill came it had tacked on to it an extra hundred dollars. Here is a copy of his one payment fixed-price contract.

SEPTIC TANK CONTRACT

Proposal submitted to: *Charles Daniels*

We hereby submit specifications and estimates for: *$4,200⁰⁰*

This price includes all materials to be furnished by our company, beginning from the septic tank and proceeding out to the fields. We will adhere to all specifications listed on the county permit pertaining to the septic system installation, up to the rough grade and inspection. The system will then be approved by the Fairfax County Health Department.

All work will be performed and completed within a reasonable amount of time providing that weather permits and materials are readily available.

We propose hereby to furnish material and labor - complete in accordance with above specifications, for the sum of:

Four Thousand two hundred _____ dollars (*4200⁰*)

Signature *Charles Daniels*

130

Kitchen Cabinets

Below I give only the top page of the contract with the kitchen cabinet supply company. They furnished the cabinest but did not install them; that was done by the carpenters. Many hand scribbled pages followed this top page and then these got changed and worked over. We bought various other things from this company: bathroom cabinets, kitchen sink, dishwasher, stove, refrigerator, formica counter tops, and the tub for the master bathroom. There was a contract for each of these. The usual procedure for cabinets was for them to measure the actual kitchen and then furnish a scale drawing showing all cabinets they proposed to furnish. I know of no room more difficult to plan than the kitchen. It is important to spend some time reviewing the kitchen design *after* the cabinet people have made their proposal. Our cabinets came from Canada and all dimensions were in centimeters which was a little awkward since nothing came out in even inches. I do not like a side of a stove to be part of a passageway. Someone passing can easily knock a hot pot off the stove and cause an accident. There should be at least one cabinet and some counter-top between the stove and the passage and I had shown this in my kitchen plan. Seeing an opportunity to offer more cabinet space, the kitchen cabinet people put in a larger cabinet than I had wanted. This indeed gave more cabinet space but it also restricted passage through the back door more than I wanted. It functions okay, but it is not quite the entrance I had designed and wanted. I mention this here to show how easily little things can slip by in the kitchen plan. I could have had exactly what I wanted at a little less cost. Below is a copy of the top page of the kitchen cabinet contract.

KITCHEN CABINET CONTRACT

To: Mr. and Mrs. Daniels

Description

NEFF, 403, Low Pressure, Almond, Fawn
Trim

Total cabinetry as per proposal	4085.12
25% discount	-1021.28
	3063.84
Tax	122.55
Delivery	245.10
Total	3,431.49

Terms: 1348.09 upon signing
2083.40 upon delivery

Accepted: _____ Date: _____

Ceramic Tile

Brownie, the tile contractor, had some people working for him who did the actual tile work at our house. He had to resubmit his first bid to delete the tile for the downstairs bathroom since we had decided not to finish that room. Although he did not show it in his bid terms, he asked verbally to make a draw when he had finished the upstairs bathrooms, even though he still had the entrance foyer to complete. When he finished the entrance foyer I had a date to meet him and give him a check but he never showed. I intended to mail the check to him but somehow it all got lost in the pace of things. I did not hear from him, so one day I called and told him I had no record of paying all the money I owed him. he said he would look into it, but sometime later there still had been no phone call from Brownie. I called again and got his secretary. She pulled my file and said, "Mr. Daniels, this account is closed and we have been paid in full." She insisted that the account was fully paid. I did not pursue it any further and I still don't know exactly what happened. A copy of Brownie's fixed-price bid follows.

CERAMIC TILE CONTRACT

Proposal submitted to:
Mr. Daniels

We hereby submit specifications and estimates, subject to all terms and conditions as set forth on both sides, as follows:

Installation of ceramic tile mastic walls, mud floors, Foyer epoxy installation. Walls 4 x 4 Bright glaze, floor 4 x 4 Krystal, walls and floors - White.

Areas:
Main floor-Entry foyer, Bath w/tub
Master bath w/platform tub and shower

We propose hereby to furnish material and labor - complete in accordance with above specifications, for the sum of:

Two Thousand Nine Hundred Ninety Four and 30/100 dollars

($2994.30)

Signature _____

Concrete Finishing

The concrete finishing was another low overhead operation. The finisher showed up on the job simply at the request of Wells. There was the lead man and several helpers, and together they placed and surfaced the concrete. They furnished the wire mesh reinforcement and Wells ordered the concrete. When almost all the concrete was delivered, the lead man eyeballed the amount of concrete still needed and sent word back with the truck driver for one more load in the amount estimated. That way there is never far too little or far too much concrete. First the concrete is raked to the desired floor level and roughly finished. After a several hour wait while it sets up, the concrete can be troweled to the final finish. There was no written contract for this work but the handwritten billing given below shows how the job was charged. There was another similar billing in the amount of $763.50 to finish the garage and screened porch floor, bringing the total for the concrete work to $2,066.50.

CONCRETE FINISHING
(billing)

To: Charles Daniels

Re: Place and finish concrete basement

Finish basement 2462' at 50¢ per ft   1231⁰⁰

3 Rolls wire mesh at $15⁰⁰ per roll   45⁰⁰

2 Sils 3 feet 6 feet 9 feet at $3⁰⁰ per ft   97⁰⁰

                              Total $1303⁰⁰

Drill Well

Wells recommended that I go with a well driller with whom he had many past favorable experiences. I suggested to him the contractor who had drilled the well for our previous house. Wells said, "That's fine by me but you will pay one or two thousand dollars more." So I accepted Wells' recommendation. Two men arrived with a huge brand new drilling rig and set up on the spot marked by the county. The county health department is much involved with well drilling, and the contractor took on the problem of county inspections. The drilling rig was on the lot only overnight. By evening of the second day they were gone. Below is their billing which was the only paperwork involved.

Custom Drilling   Experienced Drillers

WELL DRILLING
(billing)

To: Mr. Charles Daniels

220' @ 8.00 $1760.00

60' casing

15 g.p.m.

Well Pump and Water System

Wells got a verbal fixed-price bid from his usual water system contractor and relayed it to me as a reasonable bid. We gave a "go-ahead" based on a verbal quotation. Here was literally a one man show. There were no helpers, only one man and a truck. He furnished all materials including the pump, electrical wiring, underground water pipe, electrical controls, and piping needs to install it all. He dug the pipe trench deep enough to avoid freezing. After extending the trench from the well to the house, he punched through the basement wall and laid the piping. When finished, he fired up a portable generator (it was one of those days when the house power was out), checked out the system, and left, all in one day. He was an ex-Navy chief and you could get along with him as long as you agreed with him. There was the right way, the Navy way, and his way. I would have enjoyed seeing the sparks fly had he and Greenie gotten together, but unfortunately that did not happen. "Charlie," he said, "I got enough of these damn pumps installed around and I'm just not gonna do this work anymore. You're lucky I'm doin' this one. Bin doin' this crap for ten years now — ever since I got out." At this point he was up to his knees in mud trying to dig a ditch that would not collapse on him and still be below the frost line. "No sir, no more o' this crap, got enough pumps installed so's I can keep busy just servicing what I already done. Got my name and phone number plastered over everything I put in. If ya ever need me, just pick up the telephone — I'll be there." Below is a copy of his single payment bill. I would like to have shown this bill in his original handwriting but it was not entirely legible. Nevertheless, it was abundantly clear to anyone who interprets handwriting that here was no shrinking violet.

Pump Service And Repairs		Ditch Trenching
	Well Pump and Water System (billing)	

To: Wells

For: new home - Charles Daniels

---

1 3/4 H.P. 230 V 10 EJ Goulds Sub. well pump + controls

1 Wx 203 Well x tral water tank, all materials, ditching and installation $1450⁰⁰

1 5 year Goulds Sub Pump Insurance Policy

Total Due $1450⁰⁰

Central Vacuum

The central vacuum contractor had an office and working crews. The bossman arrived one day on my telephone request, and to gether we walked through the up and downstairs. About ten minutes after he arrived, he pulled out a brochure describing this central vacuum system and scribled $835 on it and handed it to me. That was his contract. Talk about low overhead! I would estimate it took two men one day's work to do the whole job. Under the fixed-price contract, they provided all labor and materials.

Central vacuum systems are very handy. The vacuum power package is powerful and is remotely located, in our case in the garage. The feature I like is this: the air filter (located at the power package) is very course and only picks up bulk objects, but the remainder (including dirt and fine dust) is exhausted to the *outside* of the house. In a regular vacuum cleaner, the fine dust is exhausted *into* the house. Since I have nothing in the way of a contract to show, I reproduce below the billing for the job.

CENTRAL VACUUM
(billing)

To: Mr. Wells

Description	Price	Amount
5 Valve syst + #26 unit	750 00	
One power brush	85 00	
		835 00

Terms: 835.00 price for vac system W/5
      vals. size 26 unit, cleaning set and
      hose 40/60

      Daniels Residence

Roof Gutters and Downspouts

I had dealt with this contractor before as he had installed the gutters and downspouts on our previous house. Our agreement to proceed was a telephone conversation. Therefore there was no written contract and our verbal agreement was on a dollar per foot of gutter and downspout. Below I include his billing because it tells how he priced the job and gives all the figures. The crew arrived in the morning and left after completing the job early in the afternoon.

ROOF GUTTERS AND DOWNSPOUTS
(billing)

To: Charles Daniels

Description	Unit Price	Total
Job: Daniels Residence		
Furnished and installed .032 brown seamless aluminum 5" gutter with 2" by 3" downspouts and splash blocks for the entire new house.		
233' Gutter (5")		
71' 2" x 3" Downspout		
304' Total footage @ $2.00 per foot		$608.00
35' 3" x 4" Downspout @ $3.00 per foot		105.00
4 Splash blocks @ $5.00 each		20.00
Total labor and material		$733.00

Foundation Dampproofing

This contractor responded from Wells' phone call and there was no written contract. Wells said that he would do the job for about $100 and that it would be the best $100 we would ever spend in our lives. He arrived with his truck, sprayer, and a tank of bituminous dampproofing, sprayed for about an hour and left for another job. Here is a copy of his billing.

FOUNDATION DAMPPROOFING
(billing)

To: Wells

Description	Unit Price	Total
Foundation Dampproofing at:		
Daniels Residence		100.00
1000 sq. ft. @ .10/sq. ft.		

8

Moving In, Almost Hooray!

January 2. Well, well, the day did come and we did move in. It was fun and the culmination of something big, unfinished and exhausting —but big. The movers arrived early in the morning. We were ready for them. We were only moving two miles from the rented house to the new house and the movers were local. Madeline had made the arrangements and it turned out to be a cool dry day without complications. There was a covered van and four healthy men. Two loads did the job and they were gone, leaving us in the midst of a confusion of boxes and furniture. It did not take long to figure out that we were tired, alone and happy. At last, the first night in our dream house.

The sun came up the next day even though we did not yet have an occupancy permit. As you read earlier, the occupancy permit came weeks later after a little push and pull with the county inspector.

As much as we wanted to work on our own things at the new house, the next day found us back at the rented house cleaning up, finally leaving it "broom clean" as our rental contract required. Realizing that rentals happened to be "hot", Madeline advised our friendly landlord to put an ad in the paper, which she did. While we were cleaning up, several potential renters came and Madeline showed them the house. We relayed the information to the landlord and before we left, the house was once again rented.

Back at the new house we started to place furniture into rooms that had never before seen a chair, a bed or a sofa. There is a strange feeling when you watch the actual furniture going into places planned for them months ago. It never fits exactly as envisioned. A twist here and there and the awkwardness starts to disappear.

For the first time in our lives there was too much furniture in the house. We picked, chose and fitted, and whatever furniture was left over ended up stored in the basement. Madeline is a "string-saver" and I'm a "thrower-outer." At day's end, I looked at the store of furniture in the basement and said to Madeline, "Do you realize that I have actually moved that stuff twice now, just so I can move it once more to the dump?" She didn't think it was funny. Another thought was tugging somewhere in her mind. "It's too good to take to the dump," she said, "we're going to give it to the Goodwill outfit."

On February 7, the contractor who furnishes light fixtures finally showed up with permanent fixtures. He took down all the temporary fixtures installed long ago and replaced them. Still he was unable to obtain the light over the master bathtub. We subtracted the cost of the missing fixture and paid the balance. It was hard to believe we had ordered the fixtures back in September.

This was the only contractor to grossly mis-time his services and supplies.

When is a house completed? It's the eternal question that can never be answered. I suppose a lot depends on what you see and how you feel about it. Our house was certainly not yet completed. On the other hand, everything that had to function was working. With some exceptions, the inside of the house only needed decorating. Ceilings throughout the house were painted with a final coat but walls and trim were only primed. The kitchen and bathrooms were painted with two coats of enamel and were fully serviceable. Madeline would want these papered, but until she made her selections for the interior decor, they would remain in fine shape. To answer the question directly, I don't think I have ever seen a house that was completely finished.

So it boiled down to priorities and we had some beauties. The well, ah yes, the well! Many people think in terms of a good one or a poor one. But wells are elusive things and each has a personality of its own. Some produce crystal clear noncorrosive water from the start. It is more likely though that a well, especially a new well, will produce some contaminants in the water. When a well is first drilled (these days they are almost always drilled) the ground surrounding the well shaft is disturbed and the disturbed earth produces dirt, mud, sand, sulpher or anything else it contains. (Would you believe gas? How about Perrier water?) This shows up in the water pumped into the house. Further, each time the pump is turned on, it causes swift local currents deep in the well which erode or disturb the well walls and this produces more contamination. After a while, perhaps a year, the ground erosion proceeds to unnoticeable proportions, and the water becomes less contaminated. When a well contractor asks, "Do you want your well pumped?" he is usually referring to the above condition and he is suggesting that the initial muddy situation be reduced by steady pumping for a few days before installing the permanent pump and hooking it up to the house.

The water from our well was very muddy so I attached a hose to a fitting on the water storage tank where the water line from the well first enters the house, and let it run for several days on end. This reduced but failed to eliminate the muddy water problems. I bought a "whole house" water filter at Sears and installed it in the water line. It also helped, but failed to give us satisfactory results. Maybe it seems like a minor problem while sitting comfortably and reading this book, but believe me, when the bathtub water is muddy and your wife refuses to step in to bathe, that's not the end of it — she lets you know that it's *not* all right! I use the shower myself and there the problem is not so obvious. Immediate solutions to this, including water purifiers, may be effective but they may also be expensive. Having been through this before, my preference was "patient persistence" until the well cleared itself up. We used water extravagantly for the next few months and eventually the well cleared itself up. Now I don't need the Sears filter, although it is still in place and working.

I asked the county inspector if his analysis would reveal any chemicals or other such problem contaminants in the water. He indicated that only the bacterial contamination is checked by the county. Mineral contamination is controversial and the county may not especially want to become involved. Not a very good picture for the owner. We received the approval of our water supply from the county based on a satisfactory bacterial count.

Practical problems with the water supply from a well include items like mud, or "turbidity." When pumped into the house, the water tends to clog delicate controls such as toilet and furnace humidifier valves. In addition, color stains on sinks and toilets attributable to chemicals in the water may appear. The chemical constituents in well water change from month to month and may reach objectionable levels especially during spring. As you can see, the subject of wells can be tricky business. Their problems and personalities deserve a separate book and we can't cover the subject here.

After moving into the house, we took care of the inside priorities first. There were only a few problems concerning the inside of the house but solving them was highly important to making our lives comfortable. For example, the carpeting developed humps high enough to trip over. The carpet installers corrected this condition by stretching the carpet. It was done without additional cost to us, but we still had to keep pushing until the job was completed.

Initially, there were no drapes or window treatments. Madeline selected miniature Venetian blinds for the bathrooms which I installed immediately. She chose vertical blinds for the windows in the rest of the house. After a little time, the supplier furnished and installed them. These blinds really do control the light from the outside and they are handsome. I tried to get Madeline to develop an overall and detailed plan for decorating the interior of the house. She wants to ease into it as she lives in the house and I guarantee that there will be no comprehensive decorating plan soon. She is not at all indifferent — it's just that it's going to happen her way. So I have no exciting interior decorating plan to report on. But it is taking place slowly and it will be fun to see how this develops in the future.

Immediately pressed into service were the clothes washer and dryer. The laundry area had been planned for a double laundry tub and appropriate cabinets, but as you know, we had to settle for a single tub. I could not locate cabinets of satisfactory dimensions so I found enough plywood left from the carpenter's scraps to build what I wanted. This took a little extra time but worth it to get the laundry fully functional.

Madeline bought a few special pieces of furniture such as a circular dinette set for the kitchen eating space. It's perfect for two people and when needed, it expands to accommodate six, just as planned. At this point, the inside of the house was comfortable and I turned my attention to the outside where priority jobs were waiting.

Madeline chose vertical blinds for most of the windows in the house.

Spring comes early in Northern Virginia. By the end of March there are occasional days warm enough for some plants to start sprouting. Ahead lay the jobs of regrading (there had been settlement near the house over the winter), completing and establishing the lawn, and controlling the roof water from the downspouts.

If basement rooms are to be dry, water from the outside must be directed *away* from the house. Houses are constructed so that moisture present in the outside dirt will find its way through the basement walls and into the basement air. It would be better if the walls were completely waterproof but they are not. The inside basement walls may look dry but still be somewhat moist. To avoid this, it is best to keep the earth next to the basement walls as dry as possible. Another related condition is that basement walls tend to stay at the same temperature as the outside earth. This earth is almost always cooler than the basement air. Just as a cool glass of water sweats on its surface, so the basement walls and floor tend to sweat, especially in warm weather. Sweating is frequently mistaken for a "leaky basement." A dehumidifier and a fan to circulate the air are ways to control sweating. Another would be to insulate the basement walls. This still may not be effective if the dirt on the outside of the basement walls is laden with moisture. Temporarily, over the winter, I placed "splash plates" under each downspout to help keep the water away from the basement walls. Across the front of the house I dug a trench and placed in it a six inch drain pipe. It extended under the driveway and on to the hillside where it naturally surfaced. Each downspout was then connected to the drainpipe. I also did something similar to this in the back of the house. Now all of the roof water, and it is appreciable, is collected and carried away from the house in the drain lines giving a good start for a dry basement.

All downspouts were connected to drain lines which carry the roof water away from the house—an important step in achieving a dry basement.

The gravel turn-around area outside the garage door slopes ever so slightly away from the house. Just beyond this the ground drops off into an embankment. In the winter we do have some slick icy evenings and it would not be too difficult for a car to slide down the embankment with embarrassing results. To safeguard against this I decided to border the gravel area outside the garage with railroad ties and a split rail fence. The garage floor slopes slightly towards the garage door, and to place the railroad ties, I simply continued this slope to the edge of the gravel turn-around area. I then projected (from the positioned railroad ties) the gravel surface down the driveway. Surprise! The bulldozer operator last fall was correct. We needed two loads of driveway gravel and five loads of fill dirt. This would bring the driveway, turn-around parking area, and surrounding lawn areas up to a level consistent with the garage floor and the rest of the house. When the railroad ties were finally in place the rest of the grading became obvious. Wells had the gravel delivered. I found a nearby construction job where they were hauling away dirt. The foreman agreed to dump five loads in my yard for which he charged thirty dollars a load.

In the mid of winter, when things sometimes get pretty slippery, cars could easily get off of the turn-around area and slip (embarrassingly) down the slope. Therefore I lined the safe area with railroad ties and a split-rail fence.

I was glad to get the dirt because adjacent to the house much of the backfill had settled causing the dirt immediately next to the house to slope inward. Some of the dirt delivered was topsoil and I selected this dirt to fill around the house. Soon I would be planting foundation shrubs and the topsoil would obviously suit the shrubs better than the fill dirt.

The problem of dirt sloping against the house is a common one. I know because Madeline, on occasion, will list a house for sale where subsequently the buyer correctly claims the basement to be wet or damp. An examination of the outside frequently shows settlement of the ground causing the earth to slope inward, thereby trapping rainwater against the outside of the basement walls. Most of the time the earth was originally sloped properly. Then foundation plantings were made, followed by winter freezing and thawing which settled the earth to a reverse slope. When this condition goes uncorrected the basement ends up being damp.

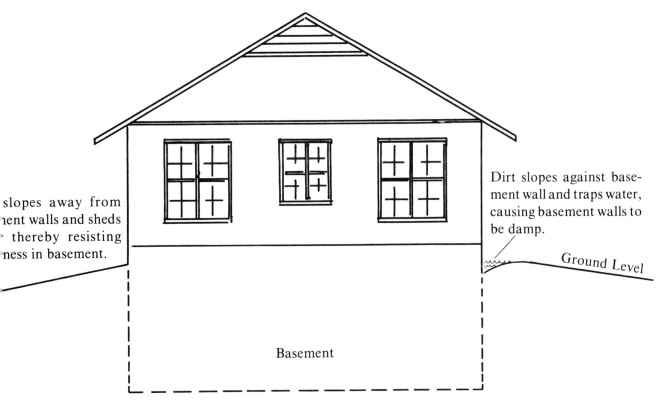

slopes away from
ent walls and sheds
thereby resisting
ness in basement.

Dirt slopes against base-
ment wall and traps water,
causing basement walls to
be damp.

Ground Level

Basement

I ordered foundation plantings from Musser Forests in Indiana, Pennsylvannia. This company sells small lots of seedlings or rooted cuttings at reasonable prices. I'm sure there are other companies that do the same. Although it takes two years for most small plants to become sizeable, the small plants usually adapt and look better in the long run. They are easier to plant and cost considerably less than the large plants. A major failure of foundation planting is selecting plants that natually grow too large. Look around your neighborhood and you will probably see what I mean. Pruning plants that want to grow larger extends their usefulness but eventually the problem shows. I prefer plants which naturally restrict themselves to an appropriate size. Books and more books have been written on this subject but here I will only explain which plants I chose and why.

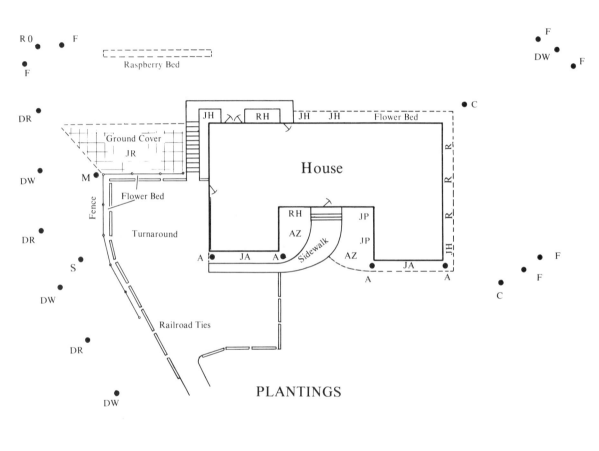

PLANTINGS

A	Alberta Spruce	JP	Japonica Pieris
AZ	Azalea	JR	Juniper Rug
C	Canadian Hemlock	M	Maple
DR	Dogwood Red	R	Rose
DW	Dogwood White	RH	Rhododendron
F	Forsythia	RO	Russian Olive
JA	Juniper Andorra	S	Spruce
JH	Japan Holly		

Along the front of the house (which shows conspicuously from the driveway entrance) I planted Andorra junipers. These plants are evergreen, grow quickly, and mature to a height of one-and-a-half to two feet. Junipers are basically a desert plant and they naturally live through wet and dry periods. They do require some sunlight, otherwise they drop much of their foliage and show unattractive woody limbs. At the front corners of the house I planted dwarf Alberta spruce because these are not only evergreen but also grow in a very compact way (require little or no shearing) and reach a mature height of only six or seven feet. At one of the previous homes that I built, I planted Canadian hemlock trees at the corners of the house. It was not long before these natural beauties had exceeded the height of the roof line. By then it was almost impossible to contain them by pruning. Within the "U" section of the front of the house I selected azaleas, rhododendron, and *Pieris japonica*. These are all evergreen varieties. I chose rhododendron that mature at a height of about four feet and I planted them under windows. The windows are four feet above the ground and these plants will never grow high enough to obscure them. Here the roof was only a bit over eight feet high and had a two foot overhang. This restricted the amount of rain adjacent to the house foundation. For this reason I planted the rhododendron just beyond the roof drip line to assure the plants enough rain water. I deliberately chose rhododendrons that were all the same variety so they would tend to bloom at the same time come Spring. The azaleas were also of the same variety for the same reason. Azaleas were all of the variety that tend to mature when about three feet tall but can be pruned indefinitely to a lesser height. One side of the "U" was shaded all the time and for this area I selected *Pieris japonica,* which tolerates shade. It grows to a mature height of four feet. *Pieris japonica,* likes both acid soil and a lot of mulching, the same as rhododendrons and azaleas, so I expect they will all get along together in the same bed.

On the southwest side of the house under the bedroom windows, I planted roses. Here the bed was exposed to full sunlight in the winter and partial sunlight in the heat of the summer. In a previous house I grew some very nice roses under similar conditions. Roses are not evergreen, and in my opinion, don't make good-looking foundation plantings. The house is set so that the southwest side of the house is seldom seen from the road or the rest of the yard, and I'm hoping it will be an ideal spot for roses.

At the right corner of the back of the house, I planted a Canadian hemlock tree. The roof line here is eighteen feet so it could grow pretty much as high as it wanted, although I understand that at some distant date it could possibly exceed this height. Adjacent to door entrances and to hide the   air conditioner condenser, I planted Japanese holly bushes because they hardly ever need pruning and mature at a height of about three feet. This left a long bed against the back of the house which gets full sunlight until about noon. Here Madeline could plant whatever she wanted, probably flowers for picking such as zinnias, gladiolas, clematus, and chrysanthemums.

Away from the house, at the driveway entrance and at the corners of the lawn where the mowing ends, I placed clumps of forsythia. Along the driveway is a row of trees. They are mostly dogwood and all are spring-blooming and easy to care for. The steep bank dropping off from the gravel turn-around area toward the back of the lot was hard to mow. It gets almost full sun so I planted it in rug junipers, an evergreen groundcover having a mature height of about four inches.

At the corner of the gravel turn-around area is a special Spruce tree. About two years ago Madeline and I visited our daughter and her family in the Pacific Northwest. We went on a camping trip along the shores of Lake Chelan in the state of Washington. Trees there are unbelievably unblemished and beautiful. I could not resist digging up a perfect little seedling to take home. After surviving the flight home in my suitcase I planted it in our Virginia clay, then transplanted it to the rented house and finally transplanted it again to the prominent place in the yard of our dream house. It's small but it's doing well.

Things are beginning to work now the way they are supposed to. The house is near perfect for two people. We had the bridge club over a few nights ago. All had a fine dinner and later the great-room expanded to accommodate the card tables and players very comfortably. Downstairs my workshop is taking form and I'm getting back to doing the wood craftwork I enjoy so much. My brother and his wife are coming to visit soon and there is a lovely guest room awaiting them.

The weather is getting cold again and the "frost is on the pumpkin." It's Thanksgiving time and our kids are coming home with grandkids to see our new house — all except our daughter in the Pacific Northwest. We called her on the telephone and had a bit of a reunion. She was preparing Thanksgiving dinner for her new family out that-a-way. The fire glows warmly from the fireplace. Turkey dinner hmmmmmm. Dream house off and running.

IN AND AROUND THE HOUSE

We elected to build a hot air circulating fireplace with a raised hearth. Usua[l] air is taken in through grates in the face of the hearth, warmed by circulating over the back of the hot firebox, and then exhausted back into the roc[m] through the brick openings above the fireplace. I decided to position the [air] intake grates, which are equipped with fans, in the basement near the ceilin[g] Now, when I heat my workshop (with a little wood stove) a great deal of war[m] air accumulates at the basement ceiling. This warm air is transferred upsta[irs] simply by turning the fireplace fans on.

Hose faucets should be specified to be at least eighteen inches above the ground. I have specified the eighteen inches on each house we have built but there is always one faucet that ends up near ground level. Accordingly it is impossible to get a bucket or watering can under them.

In years past eaves were boxed in (covered) and left without adequate ventilation. This invites condensation and rotting. It is advisable to provide ventilation where eaves are boxed in to prevent this condition. Here you see an almost continuous vent slot which is screened on the inside to prevent wasps and their cousins from nesting inside the eaves and the attic. Screened attic ventilators are also advisable for the same purpose.

157

APPENDIX I

Useful Sources
of Information

County Codes

These should be available from your county seat. I have found that county codes, for my county, are not available in a single bound volume. The assembled codes, I understand, would make a book about four inches thick. Zoning codes covering the sizes of lots allowed, the kinds of houses (single dwellings, town houses, etc.) allowed in each zone, house set-backs from property lines and similar matters, were readily available usually in pamphlet form for a small fee. Other codes I needed defined septic tank and drain field rquirements and I obtained these from the health deparment. Official lot dimensions and contour maps I got from the maps and charts department for a fee. One stumbling block is that counties keep their files according to legal lot descriptions (lot Z in Camelot subdivision) rather than by street address. When a lot is for sale by a real estate agent, he will have a legal description and he should also be able to help you with other detailed material you may need.

Covenants

These are restrictions set upon the area, or the particular lot you have in mind, by the previous owner who subdivided the land. Covenant requirements vary widely and must be researched before purchasing a lot. A seller is supposed to make this information available when the lot is sold but that is not when the information is needed. These restrictions may apply to such matters as tree removal, size and type of house, architecture standards, etc. Covenants are also found at the county seat but are usually included in the files along with ownership history, titles, deeds, etc.

House Construction

The U.S. Government publishes a book *Low-Cost Wood Homes For Rural America—Construction Manual.* This 112 page paperback has a good overview of house construction. It is available from the Superintendent of Documents, U.S. Printing Office, Washington, D.C. 20402. When I bought my copy it cost one dollar but the Government no longer publishes a price because of frequent changes. So you will have to write for the current price. If you live in the Washington D.C. area you may be able to pick up a copy at no cost from the Department of Agriculture's Forrest Service Publication Office.

Large home centers and hardware stores carry an array of "how-to" books that are authoritative and helpful. The Sears' booklets on plumbing and electrical wiring have been useful to me. Lumberyards have all sorts of data relating to doors, windows, and millwork, and frequently will let you look through their catalogs for specific information.

Rehabilitating Old Houses

The 270 page paperback book *This Old House* by Bob Vila and Jane Davison is an excellent "hands-on" manual about rehabbing old houses. It is published by Little, Brown and Company, Boston, Masschusetts. I bought a copy at a local book store (for $19.95). It has a good bibliography on related information.

Federal Taxes

Internal Revenue Service publication 523 *Tax Information On Selling Your Home* is free from the IRS. Tough reading but do it anyway. It tells how to defer/avoid paying taxes on the profit you receive when you sell your home. Although the 1986 Tax Act has uprooted many aspects of personal income taxes, it has left the conditions for selling your home essentially unchanged.

APPENDIX II

House Dreamer's
Checklist

Possible Reasons for Building a Home

• Improved prestige, or pride of ownership, is probably the primary reason for building a home.

• A higher standard of living for yourself and your family can be a major attraction.

• Special hobby accommodations can be had, such as a four-car garage for automobile buffs, a ceramics studio, or a music studio.

• A business and office in the home is a feasible option when constructing one's own home. Check the local zoning codes.

• A more or less secluded location can be had by careful selection of a new house location.

• For those with a growing family, larger living accommodations become necessary, and with construction of your own home you can add on at any time.

Your House and the Federal Income Tax

• For most homeowners their homes represent the single largest investment they will ever make. How you handle taxes when you sell your home has a great deal to do with whether you will benefit from your investment or not. Dry as this subject is, make the effort to understand it and work it to your advantage. Most who decide to build a new home will sell their present home to raise construction money and, in turn, become involved in the tax game.

• When you sell your home, if there is a profit you must defer paying income tax on the profit until a certain point, if you meet certain conditions. If you do not meet these conditions, you must pay tax on the profit.

• In the future, if you sell your new home you may defer taxes again and again. If it is done right, you may never have to pay tax on the profit from the sale of your home (includes profit from sale of previous homes where tax was deferred).

• When you reach age 55 or older and have a profit from the sale of your home (includes profit from the sale of previous homes where the tax was deferred), the tax law allows you to exempt up to $125,000 of the profit. Via this route you may be able to escape paying income tax on part or all of the profit from your life's largest investment. You may elect this exemption only once in your life.

• IRS publication 523, *Tax Information On Selling Your Home,* explains the

160

details on how taxes apply to the sale of your home. Condemn yourself to studying it and how these laws apply to you.

- Tax laws keep changing so be sure to keep up to date on homeowner's tax laws.

Selecting a Lot

- Is transportation from the lot to your job a problem? Check the traffic and commuting situation out during rush hour or under worst conditions. Also, are schools, shopping centers, sports facilities in the area to your liking?
- Does the lot have public water and sewer? If not, check the county codes for wells, septic tanks, and drain fields. If these items are not already approved by the county, make your lot purchase agreement contingent on county approval.
- Is county zoning suitable to your needs? Avoid building a home in an area where zoning permits lesser housing.
- In addition to county codes, are there also covenent restrictions on the lot? You real estate agent can get a statement of these for you.
- Is the lot sufficient to accommodate your desired house design and a garage too? Check the county building line set back codes.
- Do you want your new home to increase in value? Check the value of nearby homes and lots. Has their value been increasing or declining? You can this type of information from your real estate agent. Or you can go calling at a few of your neighbors-to-be. You'd be surprised what you'll learn.
- Will the lot complement the house you want to build? Are you willing to make the necessary adjustments if it doesn't? If not, keep on looking.

House Plans

- First, take a shotgun approach and sketch house plans.
- Next, get specific and discipline your sketches so that sizes, entrances, exposures, et cetera, fit your lot dimensions and conditions.
- Draw as complete a set of plans as you can. You may need help and this is where an architect comes in. For a price the architect can furnish (with your ideas) a complete set of plans to your liking. Or if your plans are fairly firm, your builder may come up with the necessary services and furnish the plans for you.
- Final plans must be complete enough to satisfy county building authorities. The lot may also be in a subdivision where covenants require approval by a local architectural committee. If a local builder does the final plans, he is usually aware of such requirements and will draw up the plans accordingly.
- After the plans have been submitted to you for approval, ask the builder if they can recommend any changes which would reduce cost. You may be able to agree on some alterations that would save money.

- Go over the final plans in detail before you give approval. Check every requirement and dimension, especially kitchen dimensions. Later, when a kitchen supplier has been selected, ask him to check the kitchen layout and dimensions and consider his suggestions.
- Before you give final approval to the house plans, and the builder's price for building the house, try to resolve not to make any changes during construction. If you do, you will likely pay extra. There will probably be some changes made during building, but it is best not to plan on it.

Selecting a Builder

- Theoretically, any maverick can charge ahead, hire his own subcontractors, and build his own house. On the other hand, a reputable local builder in the course of business has researched the best local suppliers, has arrangements with reliable subcontractors, has a working knowledge of local codes—the list goes on. Unless you are already in the building business, think twice about doing all these tasks on your own.
- Unfortunately, bankruptcy is not uncommon with builders. There is no sure way of your eliminating this risk, because you will probably have no direct knowledge of a given builder's financial health. Ask questions, keep your eyes open, and make your own best assessment.
- Find two or three local builders of good reputation who are building in your area. Find a house that each is building and talk with the carpenter or foreman. It will take only a minute to determine whether he respects the builder. Seek out houses these builders have constructed and chat with the owners. Would each owner recommend his builder to build your house?
- Ask each builder about his proposed or preferred contractual arrangement. You will probably prefer one arrangement over another.
- Ask each builder to furnish a cost estimate and completion date estimate. If you have complete plans, the builder may be able to provide these estimates quickly, but incomplete plans pose a problem. If so, ask each builder to bid on a proposal basis, that the plans would be completed according to his understanding of your discussions and explanations. The resulting estimates may not be final, but they should be good enough for you to make a decision.
- Based on the above, make your builder selection, complete the house plans, work out the contractual arrangements (if you haven't already), and shake hands.

Construction Loans

- Arrangements for construction loans are so varied that a good checklist for them probably can't be written. Do not, however, embark on building a custom house without some of financial reserve over and above the construction loan or the builder's cost estimate.

• Because it reduces some of the owner's risk, the author prefers an arrangement where the owner pays all expenses as they arise. Another more common arrangement is to pay a number of lump sums (called "draws") to the builder as building progresses.

• If you are taking a loan from a bank, a savings and loan, or other financial institution, you will have to meet their requirements, which vary from bank to bank. Your builder and your lot real estate agent may have some suggestions. Shop around.

• The bank will probably require you to own your lot outright before they will grant you a construction loan.

• The bank probably will not grant a construction loan on a house if the house is to be built incomplete.

• Frequently, when construction is completed, the construction loan is converted over to a conventional home loan. If you go this route, you will have to qualify for the construction loan as well as the conventional home loan. You will have to show financial resources as well as the ability to make monthly payments before the bank will loan the construction money. Each bank has it's own rules, policies, loan programs, and interest rates.

• You will also have to pay for insurance and county taxes. Sometimes the bank will include these in your loan.

• When you make your cost estimate for your house, be sure to include the cost of the construction loan (interest and loan fees) as these will not be included in your builder's construction cost estimate. You need to estimate, plan, and provide for the total cost of the project plus some reserve funds.

Helping During Construction

• Some owners want to have little to do with their house during construction. This is all right but the builder must be made aware of it. You must, however, be prepared to accept his decisions, and there are hundreds of decisions to be made during building. Remember, changes after the fact will cost you extra.

• Most owners want to participate in decisions during building. You will get more of what you want this way. But remember, your builder is the boss, not you. Develop a respectful rapport with your builder from the start. Try to do everything you can through him. When it is necessary to make decisions without him, tell him about it at your earliest convenience. Avoid making changes; they cause confusion, increase costs, and make for delays.

• Your builder will ask you for your decisions on many things, such as the color of the roof shingles, the kind of brick to use, the color of the bathroom tile, the color of the kitchen floor and counter tops, and so forth. Cooperate by making these decisions early so that any delays won't be attributed to you, and so that your builder can proceed in an orderly manner.

• When your builder says he has obtained an occupancy permit from the county and that it is time for you to move in, conduct what it is call a "walk-through inspection." Check every faucet, door lock, drain plug, toilet . . . and everything else. Be sure you are thorough because defects you miss can easily get lost at this stage and end up being "your" problem. Present your builder with a written list of things to be corrected or finished. This will bring any remaining problems out into the open and provide a basis for final settlement.

• The bank will require a "release of liens" from each major subcontractor and the builder before making a final settlement on their loan. Each state has different laws regarding liens on houses. It is probably a good idea for your builder to provide you with a release of liens document even if you do not have a bank loan.

• You are not supposed to move into your new house before the county inspector issues an occupancy permit. Different counties have different rules. The county's interest is to see to it that their codes have been met and that the house is safe for occupancy. The occupancy permit does not mean that your house has been completed.

• Your best position is to have the builder complete the house in every detail before you move in. This, however, seldom happens, so it behooves you to have a written list of items to be corrected or adjusted. Once you move, the house is not as available to workmen and your interest turns to surviving in, adjusting, and enjoying you new environment.

• Don't let the nitty-gritties eat you up. Look around. You have a beautiful new home that could last a lifetime. Take time to enjoy it!

INDEX

House Plans

Here is your opportunity to purchase detailed building plans used to actually construct the house described in this book. You are free to use these plans in any way you wish; to build your own home, study them to learn precisely how the house in this book was constructed, or change them to better suit your own needs.

A complete set of these plans consists of <u>four</u> drawings 24″ × 36″ and are chockfull of details and information. Drawn by the hand of this book's author, they <u>incorporate the changes</u> for improvement that he would make if he were to build the house again. For one set of plans, send your check or money order in the amount of $49.95 to the address below. After initial order, additional sets for $14.95 each.

Send your check or money order to:

Charles Daniels
Box 1406
Yorktown, Virginia 23692

All <u>Postage</u> and <u>Handling</u> costs included in purchase price.
Virginia residents add 4½% sales tax.
Include name and address with your order.